# GOSPEL *on* **STAGE**

## *Original Inspirational Plays*

Elaine Petry

authorHOUSE®

*AuthorHouse*™
*1663 Liberty Drive*
*Bloomington, IN 47403*
*www.authorhouse.com*
*Phone: 1 (800) 839-8640*

*Published by AuthorHouse  06/28/2017*

*ISBN: 978-1-5246-9812-6 (sc)*
*ISBN: 978-1-5246-9813-3 (hc)*
*ISBN: 978-1-5246-9811-9 (e)*

*Library of Congress Control Number: 2017910112*

*Print information available on the last page.*

*Any people depicted in stock imagery provided by Thinkstock are models,*
*and such images are being used for illustrative purposes only.*
*Certain stock imagery © Thinkstock.*

*This book is printed on acid-free paper.*

*King James Version (KJV)*
*Public Domain*

**To Elaine**

We've shared so much laughter, shared so many tears. We have a spiritual bond that grows stronger each year. Though we're sisters by birth, God always knew from the start that He would fashion us as warriors and make us sisters by heart! Preach the Gospel always. If necessary, use words.

Love,
Your Sister Lucille

## DEDICATED TO THE MEMORY OF

My beloved sister, Lucille Price.
I am so blessed that God loaned you to me on the trail
of life. You taught, mentored, motivated, preached,
protected, led, loved, and left nothing undone.

# INTRODUCTION

After thirty-five years of writing, producing, and acting in community plays, I have recognized and used the stage as a powerful tool of evangelism. I gathered people of all ages and walks of life from various small churches, large cathedrals, local organizations, one on one solicitation, or anyone who answered an advertisement. With the producer, administration and a director in place, the last requirement was performers who had a positive mindset, a humble spirit, and some indication of raw talent.

Perhaps your church or organization would like to raise funds or just have fun staging a play. There is a plethora of self-help material online and in the library for acting, directing, and producing a stage play. My favorites throughout the years are: Play Directors Survival Kit by James W. Rodgers and Wanda C. Rodgers, The Technique of Acting, and The Art of Acting both written by Stella Adler.

Whatever the status of your theatrical background, whether novice, experienced, or veteran, you will become an evangelist as you share the Gospel Onstage.

# CONTENTS

# THE BEAUTY CONSULTANT

# THE BEAUTY CONSULTANT

*⁸Give unto the Lord the glory due unto His name: bring an offering and come into His courts. ⁹O worship the Lord in the beauty of holiness: fear before Him all the earth. Ps. 96:8, 9*

The Beauty Consultant is a skit where Pamela, the hostess, has invited four of her friends to attend a party where they will attain "beauty" from the inside out. Assuming that they will be solicited to buy beauty products, her friends wait in anticipation for the Beauty Consultant to arrive.

They are surprised when she ministers to each one with a scripture in their distinct area of need.

## CAST OF CHARACTERS

**PAMELA**　　The perfect hostess. Elegant, articulate, gracious.

**JORGETTE**　　Attractive, life loving spunky divorcee

**ERNIE**　　Financially burdened, but faithful and God fearing

**TINY**　　Comical, witty, clever, down to earth. Overweight and always eating.

**KATIE**　　Emotionally abused housewife and mother

**BARAKA**　　The Beauty Consultant, servant of God

# THE BEAUTY CONSULTANT

(Pamela proudly straightens a flower in a flamboyant bouquet display as she places the vase in the center of a small table. She rearranges a chair or two as she takes a last approving glance around her room. The doorbell rings. She quickly checks her watch before scampering to the "door")

PAMELA
Jorgette! Always on time!

JORGETTE
Hey girl! (They hug)

PAMELA
Come on in. (Beckons her inside)

JORGETTE
Is there anything that I can do to help?

PAMELA
Everything is all set! (Gestures to depict the exquisite preparations).

JORGETTE
What kind of party is this anyway? I want to let you know right now that I just come to these make-up and jewelry parties for the food. (Strutting) I am    beautiful and I don't need no help.

PAMELA
(Laughing) You go, girl. But it's much more than that. She just calls herself the Beauty Consultant. It's her ministry. You're going to love it.

JORGETTE
We'll see. Where is everyone else? Don't you just hate CP time?

PAMELA

Actually, I hate that expression. (The doorbell rings) They're here now. (Answers the door.) What's this? Did you all ride together?

ERNIE

(Three friends enter) Yes!! Katie drove. And this woman is a menace on the road.

KATIE

(Apparently sad) You should talk. (Bumping into Tiny)

TINY:

She appears to be a menace walking as well. (Gets food before sitting)

PAMELA

(Chuckles) Make yourselves comfortable, everyone. Our Consultant will arrive shortly.

ERNIE

(Pulling her invitation out of her bag) What kind of party is this anyway? (Reading) "The Beauty Consultant prayerfully invites you to a life changing experience. Beauty from the inside out – at your fingertips. Contact your hostess, Pamela Praise for more information." What product is used to make me beautiful from the inside out? An antacid? A laxative? (Laughing at her own joke)

PAMELA

I don't mean to be vague, but there's just no way that I can explain it. I went to a party last year and my whole life changed.

TINY

How? You didn't get **that** beautiful; you still ain't got no man. (Everyone laughs.)

JORGETTE

I don't need no man to feel good about myself. I'm beautiful on the outside of myself, within myself, and –

TINY
And you still all **by** yourself, too.

KATIE
(Moves and knocks over the flowers in the vase) Ooooh, I'm so sorry. Pamela please forgive me.

PAMELA
No harm done. Sit over here, Honey. (Moves her away from the flowers) My life really did change last year. I gave the Beauty Consultant all of your names because you are my very best friends and I want the best for you.

JORGETTE
How badly do you think that we look? Or is this one of those network, pyramid, empty your checkbook deals?

PAMELA
You know me better than that. We've been together for a long time. I went through Grade School, Middle School, High School, or College with most of you. It's not a gimmick. This is just a phenomenal experience that only God could do. It's not spooky, it's not a sales pitch, although you will need your checkbook.

ERNIE
(Slapping her knee) I knew it! These companies are all the same. I hope she has something that cost $5 or less because that is the extent of my extra spending this week. Well, every week if the truth be known.

KATIE
Oh I could lend you money if you…(picks up her purse and begins to search) I don't even think that I brought my checkbook but – (she accidentally dumps everything on the floor)

JORGETTE
Why are you so nervous? You've been a wreck since you got here.

ERNIE
(Motions to Jorgette to "chill" and speaks softly) Ixnay!

JORGETTE
What? What's wrong? (Strained and awkward silence) Katie what's wrong?
What do you all know that I don't?

KATIE
(Continuing to nervously arrange and replace the items in her purse) It's
nothing new really. It just always hurts like it's the first time.

JORGETTE
Jeff?? (Answering her own question) It's Jeff. What did he do now??

KATIE
This is a party, Jorgy. I don't want to spoil it for everyone else.

TINY
Thank you. I love you, Kate, but Jeff is not worth wasting an evening on.

PAMELA
Of course he is. He's her man, Tiny.

TINY
He's everybody's man, whosoever will have him. (Munching)

KATIE
(Expels a small gasp and wipes a tear from her eye)

PAMELA
Tiny, please!

TINY
I'm living in the real world. Have your little cry, cut your losses, and go
ahead and raise them bad kids y'all done had.

PAMELA

We care about you, Honey. You can share it if you like, but you don't have to if you don't want to.

KATIE

I told the others in the car, but well, everybody just pray for me because I don't know how much more of this I can take.

JORGETTE

Pam is right. You don't have to share because we all know that it's Jeff. He's hanging out again.

KATIE

It's not just another affair this time. He's in love. I know he's in love with someone else. I've lost him.

ERNIE

(Hugs her) Let's trust God on this one, Baby.

JORGETTE

Katie, you're always in so much pain with this marriage. Would it hurt any less if you were by yourself?

KATIE

I'm not like you, Jorgette. You don't need anyone. All five of your ex-husbands are still in love with you. You get up each day and max life out by the moment. What am I going to do trying to raise three small children alone? (Crying) I made Jeff my whole life.

TINY

That was your first mistake. Didn't you know the man was a drunk and a woman chaser when you married him?

KATIE

I wasn't saved either, Tiny. I just thought that I could change him.

TINY
That was your second mistake.

KATIE
I can't go on without him.

TINY
Straaa-rike three! (Bites into a donut)

KATIE
Like I said, I'm know I'm not strong like Jorgy, but I know that I'm too scared of God to commit suicide.

JORGETTE
You're wrong about me, Katie. And I do need someone. I needed someone every time that I got married. Then I found out that if I made Christ the center of my desires, peace and joy were mine.

PAMELA
Amen.

TINY
That's right. But again, in a real world situation, being saved doesn't plaster a smile on your face while some dead beat bum of a husband is blowing up your life.

KATIE
Be careful, Tiny. Someone may mistake that for compassion. Jorgette, why did you leave your husbands?

JORGETTE
They left me. I didn't leave them. I just didn't care. That's not right either. (As though realizing for the first time.) I should have felt something. The bottom line is still to make Christ your whole life.

PAMELA

We're all in one battle or another. We just have to keep praying for one another, because all of our battles are the Lord's. He's just building our faith.

KATIE

It just seems like everyone else handles their problems so much better than me.

TINY

No. Each trial is exclusively designed for the individual. Your trial will bring YOU closer to Christ. See, if I had your situation, it wouldn't be a trial for me. I'd beat Jeff, kick him out, NOT divorce him just to make him suffer, take ALL of his money, and not blink an eye.

KATIE

How do you know that you'd behave like that?

ERNIE

'Cuz that's what she did to her handicapped husband.

KATIE

Clifton is handicapped?

TINY

He is now. So you see, handling Jeff is a no brainer for me. What if you had my trial, where my only son is a grown man and will never be more that 7 ½ in his mind? He's severely challenged. Or what about Pam? She looks healthy but has to take shots for her arthritic pain.

PAMELA

I praise God. It could be a lot worse.

TINY

Ernie and her old man BOTH just lost their jobs. Which is a good reason to not ever marry someone with whom you work.

ERNIE

For real, but something good is coming though. Our breakthrough is coming through!

PAMELA

(Doorbell is heard) Oh, she's here!

TINY

Finally!

PAMELA

(To Baraka) Hi! Come on in!

BARAKA

Hello, everyone! (She carries a small attaché case)

JORGETTE

Where are the products?? In that small bag?

BARAKA

Yes, they are. (To Pam) Are you ready for me to start?

PAMELA

You may start whenever you like.

BARAKA

Well let us begin. Welcome to all of you this evening. My name is Baraka Benir and I am the Beauty Consultant. Benir is my maiden name, for I have never married. My father was French and my mother was African. They met in the United States, fell in love, married, had me and saved me the cumbersome task of becoming a U. S. citizen through the Immigration Department. (Smiles and chuckles from the ladies)

Both of my parents were missionaries in South America. One glorious morning when the three of us were traveling downriver, they were viciously slaughtered by a hostile tribe. I was six years old.

Their bodies were found ashore, along with an empty canoe. For two weeks after that, the others in our party searched for me. The wife of one of the missionaries found me sleeping under a tree one day while she was picking fruit twenty feet from the camp. Being childless, she and her husband raised me as their own. I called them Momtwo and Dadtwo. They were mother and father to me, but never let me forget the brave and awesome servants that my parents were in the Kingdom of God.

However, the whole ordeal left me scarred and bitter. I hated God. I rebelled and ran away in almost every country my foster parents traveled to. I did not understand how God could let such a horrible thing happen to a little girl. Frankly speaking, I thought that He hated me. Every time that I would mess up, Momtow would always hug me and whisper "the pain of your loss is manifested through your behavior, but I know that you are beautiful inside, for true beauty comes from the heart." That used to make me even more frustrated. Counselors you ask? I saw a million of them.

When I was 18, we were traveling in Africa and I decided to quit the missionary field. Why should I continue to serve a God who had only caused me heartache and loss? The sentence was barely out of my mouth when I became very sick. A fever raged through my body and I was not expected to live through the third night of the illness.

My foster parents were praying on each side of me. I heard my Momtwo say, "not yet, Lord. You know how beautiful you made her. Let her finish what you sent her to do."

Immediately, I was taken back twelve years to that day on the river when I was six. All three of us, my natural parents and me, were raised from the canoe by an unseen force. (Becoming teary) We saw what happened from the air. I tell you that my parents never felt the torture of that slaughter because they were taken within the second that the arrows pierced their bodies. The attackers never saw me. I remembered being in such a wonderful place. A voice asked me, "will you go? Will you share what I did for you?" I said, "yes" then and in my weakened state I said yes again. "I remember Lord, I still want to go." The fever broke immediately and I have understood my mission ever since.

Ladies, I have come to tell you that though you may have losses in your life, though you may be pierced in your body with infirmities or in your spirit with heartaches, (points up) He know all about it.

Reflect Him! When life deals its harshest blow, let the beauty of His essence flow from you that others can see and He is glorified.

TINY
That's impressive. But, what's in the case? What are you selling?

BARAKA
Ah. Key chains with engraved scriptures.

TINY
Are you serious?

ERNIE
And that makes you a beauty consultant?

BARAKA
(Smiling) Yes I am serious and yes that makes me a beauty consultant. I engrave scriptures and give them away to people like yourself. It is my ministry. It is what the Lord has me to do. It is my source of income.

JORGETTE
How can it be a source of income if you give them away?

BARAKA
I give them away for a donation. If you do not want to give a donation, that is just fine. The Lord took care of me for two weeks in the jungle and I have not had any complaints since.

KATIE
I'm sorry, but that doesn't make any sense.

13

BARAKA
I know. But (opens her case) here is one for you. And you, and you, and you, and you. (Each lady receives one)

ERNIE
Oh, thank you Jesus. My scripture is from Malachi 3:10! My husband and I have been standing on this scripture since we lost our jobs! This is confirmation, Sister. Please, take this small token of my gratitude. (Gives her five dollars) Hallelujah!!

BARAKA
It is great my sister of faith because it is all that you have.

ERNIE
(To Pam) Did you tell –

PAMELA
No. I certainly did not.

TINY
Healing! Thank you, Jesus. (Writing a check) Here, Baby! I know God sent you to give me this Word!

PAMELA
Yes! Yes! A double portion! Victory is Mine! (hands Baraka cash)

JORGETTE
Romans 8:1! No condemnation! I know that's mine. I'm forgiven and I'm free! I'm yours, and I'm going to keep on living with joy. Thank you, Jesus. (Writes a check)

KATIE
(Taking the chain and reading the scriptures) There's two on here. 1 Sam. 17:47 and 2 Chr. 20:15. Who's got their bible?

PAMELA
There's one on the table. (She gets it and hands it to Katie)

KATIE

1 Sam. 17:47 reads "And all this assembly shall know that the Lord saveth not with sword and spear: for the battle is the Lord's, and He will give you into our hands.

PAMELA

We were just talking about that! You know, the battle is the Lord's.

KATIE

(Excitedly) I know. The other one says, "And he said, Hearken ye, all Judah, and ye inhabitants of Jerusalem, and thou king Jehoshaphat, thus saith the Lord unto you, Be not afraid nor dismayed by reason of this great multitude; for the battle is not yours, but God's."

BARAKA

It appears that there is a great battle of salvation for someone close to you. Right now, it looks like Goliath. But God just handed you a stone. It is His battle. Whoever the devil is trying to steal, whatever the devil is trying to take from you, do not be dismayed. Just praise Him. It is His battle and He is not lacking in the department of war. So come! Let us praise and worship Him. Sing unto Him!

Song(Optional):

KATIE: Yes Lord, I trust you. I will wait on You!

Choreographed dance / song (Optional)

# THE BEAUTY CONSULTANT

# SET

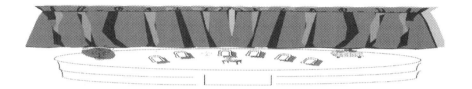

# PROP LIST

**Tray of celery/carrots/dip/chips (for table)**
**Six cups (For beverage on table)**
**Pitcher of beverage**
**Six tea cups/saucers (for table)**
**Napkins**
**Cutlery**
**Centerpiece**
**Elegant table cloth**
**Flowers in vase**
**Bible**
**Check Books**
**Pocketbooks**
**Six Key Chains**
**Attaché Case**
**Five pocketbooks**

# THE HYPOCRITES

Two loveable sisters who love to hate and who redefine Hypocrisy, overlook repentance at a critical time.

**$25 in advance**

**Saturday, November 7, 2015  7:00 PM**

*Doors open at  6:45pm*

**Any Organization**

**100 Percent True and Funny**

**Any Town, Worldwide 88888**

*Call 555 309-5577 for more information*

Two sisters, Maggie and Myrtle Johnston, are devout Christians...on Sunday! But Monday through Saturday the church has its place, as long as it is far from them. Whether it is a funeral, wedding, or just their twisted imagination, they can find the absolute worst in everyone.

Much to their surprise, the world as they know it is turned upside down when all of the true believers disappear and the sisters are left behind. They think that God is hard of hearing when they try to cut a deal with Him to let them into Heaven.

# HYPOCRITES
## Cast of Characters (Alphabetical)

| | |
|---|---|
| Brother Foe | An Usher |
| Cammy | Child of Deacon and Sister Ladychaser |
| Deacon Ladychaser | Adulterous member of the church |
| Grim Reaper | Takes Maggie/Myrtle to hell |
| Jack Miller | Loving caring husband of Nancy Miller |
| Jeff Tepid | Reporter, fiancé of Shelby Biddle |
| Jessie Mae | Oldest mentally abused daughter of Myrtle |
| Jimmie Lee | Child of Myrtle |
| Jonny Mae | Child of Myrtle |
| Maggie Johnston | Hypocritical and mean church woman, sister of Myrtle. |
| Myrtle Johnston | Hypocritical and mean church woman with three children |
| Nancy Miller | Sickly Co-worker of Maggie Johnston |
| Pastor Goodword | Good and honest man of God. Still hopes the best for the Johnstons |
| Shelby Biddle | Daughter of Sister Biddle, engaged to reporter Jeff |
| Sister Biddle | Hard working widowed Church Secretary, mother of Shelby and Tasha |
| Sister Goodword | Humble loving wife of Pastor Goodword |
| Sister Ladychaser | Faithful wife of Deacon Ladychaser has newborn and unseen children |
| Sister Overton | Overweight Church caterer |
| Sister Wrong | Bitter church member who reacts to the Johnston sisters' cruelty |
| Sister Wurse | Hidden Instigator who enhances Sister Wrongs bruised feelings |

# HYPOCRITES
## Prop List for Characters
### *In order of Appearance*

| ACT/ SCENE | CHARACTER | PROP/SET | COSTUMES (NC – no change) (CC –change clothes) |
|---|---|---|---|
| **Prologue** | Jeff Tepid | Microphone | Dark Suit (NC) |
| **1-1** **1ˢᵗ church** **scene** | Myrtle | Bible, announcements | Church clothes (CC) |
| | Sis. Biddle | Bible, Purse | Church Clothes (CC) |
| | Pastor Goodword | Bible | Dark Suit (CC) |
| | Maggie | Bible, Purse | Church Clothes (CC) |
| | Sis. Goodword | Bible, Purse | Church Dress (NC) |
| | Dea. Ladychaser | Bible | Stylish Suit (CC) |
| | Sis. Ladychaser | Baby, Purse, Baby Bag | Maternity Church(CC) |
| | Shelby | Bible, Purse | Church Clothes (CC) |
| | Sis. Wrong | Bible, Purse, Program | Church Clothes (CC) |
| | Sis. Wurse | Bible, Purse | Church Clothes (CC) |
| | Sis. Overton | Bible, Purse, Tote Bag with food | Church Clothes (CC) |
| | Bro. Foe | None | Black Suit (NC) |
| | Jack Miller | Bible, Pill Bottle, water bottle | Suit (CC) |
| | Nancy Miller | Bible, Purse, Handkerchief | Church Clothes (CC) |
| **1-2** **Office scene** | Maggie | Newspaper, Coffee cup | Business suit (CC) |
| | Nancy Miller | Calculator, phone, Pen | Business suit (CC) |
| | | 2 chairs | |
| | | Table | |
| | | 8 ½ X 11 Papers/folders | |
| **1-3** **Myrtle's** **Home** | Jessie Mae | Bible, Water Bottle | Jeans, Top |
| | Jonny Mae | Doll, Pillow | Stretch Jeans, Top |
| | Jimmie Lee | Truck | Jeans, Top |
| | Cammy | - | Jeans, Top |
| | Myrtle | Clothes Basket/ Nail Polish | Casual |
| | | Table | |
| | | Picture of Dea. Ladychaser | |

| 1-4<br>**Funeral** | Sis. Wurse | Picture of Nancy Miller | Black Dress |
|---|---|---|---|
| | Sis. Wrong | Red Rose | Black Dress |
| | Pastor Goodword | Black Table Cloth | Suit |
| | Lady Goodword | | Same Dress |
| | Dea. Ladychaser | | Suit |
| | Sis. Biddle | | Beautiful suit/dress |
| | Jack Miller | | Black Suit |
| | Bro. Foe | | Black Suit |
| | Maggie | | Black |
| | Myrtle | | Black |
| 1-5<br>**Wedding**<br>**Scene** | Wedding Party<br>(Transition Dance) | Tables | All Formally Dressed |
| | Shelby (Bride) - | Flowers | Gown |
| | Jeff (Groom) | Champagne glasses | Tux |
| | Maggie | Table cloths | |
| | Myrtle | | |
| | Rev. & Sis.<br>Goodword | | |
| | Sis. Biddle | | |
| | Dea. Ladychaser | | |
| | Sis. Ladychaser | | |
| | Sis. Wrong | | |
| | Sis. Wurse | | |
| **INTERMISSION** | | | |
| 2-1<br>**2ⁿᵈ Church**<br>**Scene** | Myrtle | Bibles | All in Church clothes |
| | Sis. Biddle | | |
| | Pastor Goodword | | |
| | Maggie | | |
| | Sis. Goodword | | |
| | Deacon Ladychaser | | |
| | Sis. Ladychaser | | |
| | Sis. Wrong | | |
| | Sis. Wurse | | |
| | Sis. Overton | | |
| | Bro. Foe | | |
| | Jack Miller | | |
| 2-2<br>**Street** | Jeff | Microphone | |
| | Maggie | | |
| | Myrtle | | |

| 2-3 Judgment | Roll call for afterlife…in the following order: | | |
|---|---|---|---|
| | Angel | **Book of Life** | White robe/wings |
| | Jack | | White suit/heaven |
| | Sis. Wrong | | White dress/heaven |
| | Sis. Wurst | | black /hell |
| | Shelby | | white/heaven |
| | Jeff | | black suit |
| | Sis. Ladychaser/ Baby | | white/heaven |
| | Cammy | | white/heaven |
| | Dea. Ladychaser | | black/hell |
| | Jessie Mae | | white/heaven |
| | Jhonnie Mae | | white/heaven |
| | Sis. Biddle | | white/heaven |
| | Sis. Overton | | white/heaven |
| | Rev. Goodword | | white/heaven |
| | Sis. Goodword | | white/heaven |
| | Maggie | | black/hell |
| | Myrtle | | black/hell |
| | Grim Reaper | **Sickle/Mask** | Black Cape |

# ACT I SCENE 1

(Inside the church, before service. Congregants gather, greet one another and chatter in quiet conversation. *Each conversation takes place downstage then moves gradually upstage while the next conversation moves downstage.*)

REV. GOODWORD:
(*To Sister Biddle downstage center*) Good morning Sister. Are you still in one piece this morning?

SIS. BIDDLE:
(*Chuckling*) Good morning Reverend. I don't remember my wedding planning being this much work!

REV. GOODWORD:
Well my wife is the best planner I know. Make sure you see her this week to settle anything more that the church can offer for next Saturday.

SIS. BIDDLE:
Oh you and Sister Goodword and the church's committees have already done so much. Actually, the biggest work was making her gown. We went all the way to the city to get the right buttons and hooks. This little shop downtown had anything from antique broaches to futuristic coaches. I'm really having a good time doing all of this.

REV. GOODWORD:
I know that your husband is smiling from heaven.

(*Sister Goodword approaching Maggie from behind lightly touches her arm. Maggie, from stage right, has been trying to inch closer and closer to Sister Biddle and Reverend Goodword. She pretends to thumb through her Bible. Rev. Goodword and Sister Biddle move slowly stage left still chatting quietly*)

SISTER GOODWORD:
Sister Maggie, how are you this morning?

MAGGIE:
Oh good morning, Sister Goodword. I was just deep in the Word this morning. You know we got to be ready to receive the Word by the Word.

SISTER GOODWORD:
Yes, of course.

MAGGIE:
And much as I love the Word, I hope your husband don't get carried away today. You don't have to sit up in church all day to get a message that we sometimes forget anyway.

SISTER GOODWORD:
Oh, I take notes and review them during the week. That way, you won't forget. And it really works when you apply the weeks message to your own life.

MAGGIE:
Hm. Maybe so.

SISTER GOODWORD:
Why sure! Take last week. He was preaching from...(They continue chatting as they turn 180 degrees to move upstage. Sister Goodword takes Maggie's bible from her and shows her a scripture.)

DEACON LADYCHASER:
(*Moving from stage right, Deacon Ladychaser speaks blandly to his wife*) Whatever you wanna do Rachel, it's fine with me.

RACHEL LADYCHASER:
(*Rocking baby softly in her arms*) Well right now, I want you to have an opinion. Do you want to go to my parents or not? I have to let them know.

DEACON LADYCHASER:
Sure, why not? (Sarcastically) I love son-in-law bashing.

RACHEL LADYCHASER:
See, that's what I'm talking about. We don't have to go. As a matter of fact, I'd rather not go if you're just going to go and sit there like you're from another planet and just read a magazine.

DEACON LADYCHASER:
Tell you what, Pumpkin. Why don't you go and I'll just grab a sandwich. I have some work to do from the office this afternoon anyway. It will give me a chance to get a jump on tomorrow.

RACHEL LADYCHASER:
No, I'll just call and make it another day. They understand that-

DEACON LADYCHASER:
Rachel, I insist. Just give them my best!

*(Enter downstage left Shelby with Myrtle rushing to catch up)*

MYRTLE:
Oh Shelby!

SHELBY:
*(Tries to pretend that she does not see her)*

MYRTLE:
Shelby!!! *(Catches her and pulls her to a stop)* So! Are you ready for the big wedding day?

SHELBY:
Good morning, Miss Myrtle. Yes, I am. Excuse me, please. *(Begins to leave)*

MYRTLE:
Uh, you know, Shelby, I didn't get my invitation to your wedding yet.

SHELBY:
It was kind of like a general open invitation to the whole congregation.

MYRTLE:
Well, that was kind of Reverend. He always did give your Momma whatsoever her little heart desired. Soooooo, this wedding kinda came up lickety split, didn't it??? One minute you's jist meetin' Jeff, and here we are monts lata and there's a weddin' in the works.

SHELBY:
*(Hands extended in puzzlement)* And what are you implying? I'm missing your point, Miss Myrtle.

MYRTLE:
Oh nun't, nun't, nun't. Listen, I saw Reverend's car over your house and I was wondering –

SHELBY:
Uh, Jessie Mae and Sasha's holding a seat for me. Excuse me. *(She leaves and speaks with Jesse Mae and Sasha who are already seated)*

SISTER GOODWORD:
Oh, Myrtle! (Who is startled...she has just stolen the announcements from the pulpit)

MYRTLE:
Good morning Sister Goodword. How you doing this morning?

SISTER GOODWORD:
Just fine. I wanted to ask you –

MYRTLE:
Yeah. I have a little something to ask you too. What's the biggest reason for the divorce rate in America?

SISTER GOODWORD:
Oh, I don't know. Christians not evangelizing and living the Word of God? Those who claim to know God not really executing the love and forgiveness that Christ shows us?

MYRTLE:
Why heck no! It's womens. Them womens who prey on ι

SISTER GOODWORD:
God forbid that such a thing should happen among the

MYRTLE:
*(Glancing deliberately at Sister Biddle)* You'd be surprisec

SISTER GOODWORD:
Sister Myrtle, I need to ask you and your sister to help c
next Saturday. Sister Overton must attend her husband
need more hands in the kitchen.

MYRTLE:
Why sure! You know you can count on me! Deacon O

SISTER GOODWORD:
Overton.

MYRTLE:
Yea. He still out wid his back?

SISTER GOODWORD:
Yes. Pastor and I have been praying fervently for him.
without the saints dropping by unannounced.

MYRTLE:
They should call first.

SISTER GOODWORD:
Their number is not published. You know, he's a ι
risky giving their number out. Sister Myrtle, can I ;
Up Committee after the wedding? The caterers wi
but we just want to leave the hall in order for the Su

**RTLE:**
course. Put me down Sister Goodword. You know I'd do anything for
er Overweight.

**TER GOODWORD:**
erton.

**RTLE:**
*they leave together)* Right.

**NCY MILLER:**
*lking in with her husband Jack stage left she suddenly sways)* Oooh!

**K MILLER:**
ey! Are you ok?

**NCY MILLER:**
e fine. *(Looks in purse)* Oh, darling, I left my medicine on the console.
ant to take it before I got out of the car.

**K MILLER:**
right here! I'll go and get it. *(He dashes away quickly)*

**GGIE:**
*rs from center stage where she has been speaking with Deacon and Mrs.*
*chaiser)*

Miller! What are you supposed to be? Sick again??

**CY MILLER:**
Morning, Sister Maggie. I'm not complaining. It's just good to be
house of the Lord.

**GIE:**
your sister, and don't give me all of that empty religious rhetoric.
s me. And I'm not killing myself doing the work of two people on

that job again while you abuse sick time. And you know I'm not at my best on Mondays and-

NANCY MILLER:
Just Mondays?

MAGGIE:
Oh you making a funny? (In her face) I'll slap some naps in your weave if you-

JACK MILLER:
Hey! Hey! What's going on here? (Gives Nancy a pill bottle and a small bottle of water)

MAGGIE:
Oh, I was just picking a bone with your wife, Jack. (Sweetly seductive) She wants to talk shop and she should have stayed home today. Some people you gotta fuss with 'em to make 'em take care of theyself.

JACK MILLER:
What you're saying may be right, but where you're saying it is all wrong. Church just isn't the place. (*To Nancy*) Come on Honey, let's get you to a seat.

MYRTLE:
(To Maggie) Hey girl! I see you eying Jack Miller.

MAGGIE:
That man is gonna be mine someday.

MYRTLE:
You go, girl.

SISTER OVERTON:
(Enters and tries to squeeze between Sister Biddle and Jessie Mae on the second row. She doesn't fit. Bro. Foe, who ushered her in quickly sees the situation and adds two chairs on the end for her)

SISTER GOODWORD:
(Stepping to the podium and opens with a song, which the congregants stand and join in)

WHAT A MIGHTY GOD WE SERVE (Traditional African folk song)

WHAT A MIGHTY GOD WE SERVE
WHAT A MIGHTY GOD WE SERVE
ANGELS BOW BEFORE HIM
HEAVEN AND EARTH ADORE HIM
WHAT A MIGHTY GOD WE SERVE

WHAT A MIGHTY GOD WE SERVE
WHAT A MIGHTY GOD WE SERVE
ANGELS BOW BEFORE HIM

We serve a mighty God. Open your Bibles to Psalm 36 verse 7. *"How excellent is thy loving kindness, O God! Therefore the children of men put their trust under the shadow of thy wings. ⁸They shall be abundantly satisfied with the fatness of thy house; and thou shalt make them drink of the river of thy pleasures. ⁹ For with thee is the fountain of life: in thy light shall we see light. ¹⁰O continue thy lovingkindness unto them that know thee; and thy righteousness to the upright in heart."*

May the Lord add a blessing and understanding to the reading of His Word. Please stand as we welcome the Shepherd of this house to the pulpit, Rev. Goodword.

REV. GOODWORD:
I love my wife. She is truly a Proverbs 31 woman. I've got to preach that sermon one day. Please, take your seats. There is only one Shepherd, the Lord Jesus Christ, and I am His sheep,. May He reign in this house today. There's a song going around in my head this morning. I want Sister Wrong to come bless us with my favorite song, "There's a Brighter Side". But first, Sister Biddle come and give the announcements this morning.

MAGGIE AND MYRTLE:
(*Out loud in shock*) WHAT!?!!!

MYRTLE:
(*To Maggie*) That's your song!!! Rev! (*Whispers loudly to Rev. Goodword, who ignores her*) That's Maggie's song!

(*They look at each other in total disbelief, then look at Sister Biddle with venomous contempt. They settle in their seats with drawn faces.*)

MAGGIE:
(*Sucks her teeth*) Don't worry little sister, I got this.

SISTER BIDDLE:
Good morning, Church. Praise the Lord! (*Congregants respond*) I said Praise the Lord this morning. Come on Church, stand to your feet and give God the glory this morning. (*Everyone stands but Maggie and Myrtle*). Now if you are physically unable to stand or mentally incapacitated that you can't stand, it's alright. But those of us that love Him and who want to praise Him this morning, stand and give God the glory! (*Maggie and Myrtle stand reluctantly*)
Let's pray. Father, thank you for waking us this morning in our right minds with health, strength, and a mind to serve you. Speak to our hearts today through your vessel and feed us that we might grow even as we gather the harvest for such a time as this. In Jesus' name, Amen.
(*Looks for the announcements on the pulpit*) (*Laughing nervously*) I know I put the announcements here, church, but they seem to have disappeared. I'm sorry, Rev. Goodword, I have another copy on my desk. But if it's alright with you this morning, I'd like to give a testimony before I get them. I know that we all have a testimony, but-

MAGGIE:
(*Getting up*) You're right about that, Bitter. I do, I do, I do.

SISTER BIDDLE:
The name is Biddle.

35

MAGGIE:

Whatever! You can sit down, now. (Sister Biddle humbly sits down)
Before I give my testimony this morning, I just want to have a TRUE word of prayer. We do have prayer warriors here, such as my sister Myrtle and myself.
*(Praying)* Giving honor to Gawd, I just wanna thank Gawd for my life. I wanna thank 'im how He's blessed me with a ten room mansion my last employer left me when he suddenly dropped dead, and I wanna thank 'Im for my current employer who I caught havin an affair and he gave me a right hefty raise to keep me quiet which I did as job security…

CONGREGANTS:

*(Congregants show disdain)* Uh- uh…..Oh no!.......Jesus! That's wrong!

MAGGIE:

*(Continuing)* and I wanna thank 'im for my sister Myrtle and her beauty and the lovely head o' hair she got and for all the gifts He done give me like tongues and stuff. And I would ask for mercy for Sister Bitter this morning that God would please teach her how to pray. Let everybody here say (pause) Amen.

MYRTLE:

(alone) Amen!

MAGGIE:

Church, we got to have love. I can truly say that I love everybody. And-and-and love is not something you just show in church. I witnessed to my co-worker by my kind words and xample of living. It not only saved her life, but it saved her soul. She sittin rite here today. Stand up Nancy. You's a walking miracle.

NANCY:

(Gasping) Oh! (Jack puts his arm around her)

MAGGIE:

She shy! Plus she not feeling that good. Y'all keep her in yo prayers.

REV. GOODWORD:
Maggie! Sister Wrong is gonna-

MAGGIE:
Really enjoy this song the way it should be sung. Thank you Reverend. I'd be glad to sing it.

REV. GOODWORD:
(Shakes his head) No flesh is getting the glory here this morning, Sister Maggie.

MAGGIE:
It ain't cause flesh done sat down. (Looking at Sister Biddle) I am truly being led by a spirit here Reverend and I got to be obedient. (Sweetly) Is that alright?? (Before he can answer) Of course it is.

(Singing off key and very badly) Words by Margaret Jenkins
THERE'S A BRIGHTER SIDE SOMEWHERE
THERE'S A BRIGHTER SIDE SOMEWHERE
I AINT GONE REST UP, TILL I FINE IT
THERE'S A BRIGHTER SOMEWHERE….

**(SOUND CUE) Baby's cry CD #_____ Track #_____**

I believe I'll sing it again! *(Everyone, except Myrtle, shakes their head and motions "no" with their hands. Some sigh, others shift uncomfortably in their seats, some just look down to discourage her)*

THERE'S A BRIGHTER SIDE SOMEWHERE
THERE'S A BRIGHTER SIDE SOMEWHERE
I AINT GONE REST UP, TILL I FINE IT
THERE'S A BRIGHTER SOMEWHEREEEEEEEEE…

REV. GOODWORD:
(Gets up and takes the microphone) Come on Choir. Give a couple of selections before the offering this morning. Just get up and give God the glory. *(Looks sardonically at Maggie)* Usher the Holy Ghost back in here.

*(Choir's first song is led by Deacon Ladychaser, who sings a song directly to Myrtle.*

REV. GOODWORD:
*(Slowly approaching the mic, he prays)*
Let us pray. Father, let the words of my mouth and the meditation of my heart be acceptable unto you. Create in me a clean heart and renew a right spirit within me. Let me be that clean vessel that is purely and solely for your use in this service. Shut down and cast out every demonic spirit attached to your people this day and let the people hear and see you and not the man who stands before them. Save them, heal them, deliver them and whatever your plan is today in their lives, we shall never cease to give you all of the glory and praise, in Jesus' name. Amen.

*(Sighs with his chin resting on folded hands. He shakes his head in awe.)*
You know, Church, I spent much time in prayer and thought for today's sermon. And I am amazed. The Holy Spirit is all knowledgeable and it just so happens that He knew what was needed this morning when I prepared something else three days ago. *(Pause)* He took me a totally different way this morning and the Lord used Sister Biddle to inspire me. *(Maggie and Myrtle react)*

Turn in your Bibles to "Revelation, Chapter 19, verse 7. (Pause) Say 'Amen' when you have it. *(Maggie and Myrtle can't find the chapter and ask Sister Biddle who turns their book right side up.) (Various ones say "Amen" denoting that they have the scripture.)*

*(Reverend Goodword continues)*

Let us be glad and rejoice and give honor-

MYRTLE:
*(Interrupting)* Amen! *(Everyone looks at her)* We found it!

REV. GOODWORD:

God bless you, Sister. Let us be glad and rejoice and give honor to Him, for the marriage of the Lamb is come and His wife hath made herself ready. *(Pause for effect)* The wife has made herself ready.

What are we doing to make ourselves ready?? Going to church? Reading and studying our Bibles – yet still pampering and worshipping our flesh? (Intensely) What are we really sacrificing here? What takes us out our comfort zone to prepare? And did you notice that the Word reads "wife"? Not his girlfriend. Not his Woman or His Boo.

She is already His wife. She already has a station and a position and a name. His wife. She's already been spoken for.
But how does she get ready? Sister Biddle told me earlier (Maggie and Myrtle have another vile reaction) that she had to go all the way in the city for buttons to sew on her daughter, Shelby's gown. And get this! She said that she was having a good time making these inconvenient preparations!

*(Myrtle fidgets, chews gum, looks at her watch constantly and talks on her cell to Deacon Ladychaser)*

Preparation will cost you something. You have to go out your way to find the most miniscule pattern that will make your garment of praise fit right, feel right, and look right.

*(Raising his voice loudly)* Come on, grab a hold of this!!!

It's rich! How are you going prepare yourself waddling in sin and rebellion? Oh don't think fornication, adultery, and other sexual sins are the only things that soil your gown, Baby. What about your hatred and jealousy that fuels your tongue? What about your hypocrisy and your pride that hardens your heart to the point where you can't even hear God anymore. What are you going to be caught doing on **YOUR** wedding day?

Will you be found ready and dressed? Or will you be SLEEPING?!!
*(Maggie is startled out of a deep sleep that she had fallen into. She jumps up and 'dances' in the spirit while Myrtle calms her down. Rev. Goodword glares at her until she sits down)*

*(Music plays softy - I Surrender All by Winfield S. Weeden)*
Get serious about where you're going, Church. Create in me a clean heart and renew a right spirit in me. That is the first step. There may be one here today that is still 'spiritually single'. You're living life according to your own righteousness. Maybe no one ever told you that our righteousness is as filthy rags. I don't know. But now is the time. Now is the time for God to cover you with the precious blood of Jesus. Back in Egypt at the Passover, was everybody without sin in the house? It was not their righteousness that saved them. He said "When I see the blood, I will pass over you, and the plague shall not be upon you to destroy you…!" What's your plague today?? Get under the blood today! Get salvation, get healing! Maybe you do know Him but you've just violated your wedding vows. Get forgiveness today. It's all free for He has paid the price with His own blood

*(Sister Ladychaser along with Jack and Nancy Miller come to the altar).*

Praise the Lord. Go in peace. Raise your right hand please.

(Maggie and Myrtle raise their left hands)

REV. GOODWORD:
Raise your other right hands please. (Maggie and Myrtle sheepishly raise their right hand) May the Lord *(Congregants repeat)* watch between me and thee *(they repeat)* while we're absent from one another. *(Congregants repeat)*

*(The congregants mingle while Maggie corners Sister Biddle)*

MAGGIE:
Sooooo! Sister Bitter, I see Reverend couldn't keep you out of his mouth this morning. Why you even inspired him. What you 'spose that's all about?

SISTER BIDDLE:
I believe that he was led of the Spirit in pleading with the people to get right with God.

MAGGIE:
Where people is at with God is not his business. My mother told him that before she passed. She was on the Committee that hired him. He's just supposed to deliver the Word and keep it rolling.

SISTER BIDDLE:
Rev. Goodword was sent by God and he preaches the truth. As a matter of fact, if your mother didn't repent of her sins and invite Jesus as her Saviour, she went straight to hell.

MAGGIE:
*(Indignant)* How dare you! Who do you think you are to judge where my Mother went? You just better make sure where you're headed. And while Reverend up there talking about wedding gowns and buttons, he forgot all about the offering bad as we need money. He's straining us tithe-paying folks with all of his shenanigans.

SISTER BIDDLE:
Well, maybe if the 'tithe-paying' folks would give more than a dollar, the church's revenue might turn around. However, Rev. Goodword seems more concerned with the salvation of souls than with dollar signs.

MAGGIE:
Well, you're so close to him, I guess you do know what he's concerned about, don't you?

SISTER BIDDLE:
Any saved Christian would have understood that message this morning, Maggie. Are you struggling with it? Excuse me, please. *(Starts to leave)*

MAGGIE:
*(Grabs her by the arm)* Wait!! Oh, I feel the spirit moving on me. Oh, Oh, Oh, *(eyes rolling back in her head)* Oh oh, cumzyda harrupmi noze

41

halleleeeeuuuuu! Oh Sister Bitter, this word is for you straight from the Lord.

SISTER BIDDLE:
*(Dispassionately)* Oh, really?

MAGGIE:
Yes. *(Trying to catch her breath, closes her eyes as if seeing a vision)* Oh yes! I see it clearly. You're to go away an-an-an and rest! I see you wi – wi – wi- with with ah ah, looks like, yes! It's your bags packed!!! The Lord says go in a hurry! Matter of fact, you should join another church. Ooooh, cumzyda harrupmi noze. Cumzyda harrupmi noze. Oh Sister Bitter, don't you understand? Do you see?

SISTER BIDDLE:
*(Flatly)* Yes. It sounded like come see the hair up your nose, which can be clearly be seen by all. As I said, excuse me. *(She walks away)*

*(Maggie grabs her compact and looks at her nose. Snatches something out, then looks long and hard after Sister Biddle. Mytle who has been chatting with several men, comes over to Maggie.)*

MYRTLE:
What's wrong?

MAGGIE:
One of these days, I'm going to step on that Bitter like a bug.

MYTRLE:
And I'm sure you'd be doing God a favor too. *(Glancing at her watch)* My goodness, Rev. Goodword tried to preach into next week, didn't he?

MAGGIE:
I heard the beginning and the ending. Child, that was the best sleep I had all week.

MYRTLE:
I don't know how you could sleep with that baby hollering. I don't know why Sister Ladychaser didn't take that child down to the nursery anyway.

MAGGIE:
Cuz they don't take animals down there, Honey. I don't know what that mess is she got wrapped up in a blanket passing it off as a baby. Tarzan's money, "Cheetah ain't that ugly.

MYRTLE:
Well, the baby takes after it's Momma cuz Daddy sure looks good to me!
*(Catching his eye)*
I'll be right back. *(Calling him)* Oh Deacon! Can I have a word with you?
*(He comes to her while Maggie corners Rev. Goodword)*

DEACON LADYCHASER:
Well, you sure are beautiful today, my sweet. What are you doing later? Can I buy you a smoothie?

MYRTLE:
*(Cooing)* Oooooh! Buy one??? You are one! *(Lowering her voice)* How you gonna get away?

DEACON LADYCHASER:
I sent her to her parents. We have the whole afternoon.

MYRTLE:
It would be nice if we had dinner in the city. When are you leaving her anyway?

DEACON LADYCHASER:
We've talked about this, Myrtle. She's pregnant. I can't leave right now.

MYRTLE:
She always pregnant it seems. Are you sure all those kids are yours?

**DEACON LADYCHASER:**
Let's just enjoy each other and not make this complicated.

**MYRTLE:**
Complicated? Are you using me?

**DEACON LADYCHASER:**
Myrtle, let it go. We always end up fighting about this and quite frankly, it's getting a little old. I gotta go. *(Although engaged in another conversation, Sis. Ladychaser has been watching him closely.)*

**REV. GOODWORD:**
*(Has been trying to get away from Maggie with no success. He has been taking steps closer to downstage center when she continues audibly)*

Yes, Sister Maggie, yes. That would be fine.

**MAGGIE:**
And you know, Reverend, everybody can't preach the way you do. You just make it plain. I mean you a little long winded but that's alright. And I really enjoyed that message so much this morning. I'm going to be sharing it with everyone!

**REV. GOODWORD:**
Well, that's good sister, I just hope-

**MAGGIE:**
*(Cutting him off and talking over him)* I just know htat Word is going to bless me all week.

**REV. GOODWORD:**
*(Pats her arm, trying to leave again)* Well, God bless you Sister-

**MAGGIE:**
*(Grabs him back)* You know, there is one thing I can say for myself – and I hate to brag – but I rarely have anything bad to say about anybody, and –

MYRTLE:

*(Ambushing him from the rear)* It was a nice sermon, Rev. I'm ready. I'm wearing my spotless gown and I'm just plain out old ready. And I'm going to spread your message all week. I'm going to preach to everyone that I meet. I'm going to –

REV. GOODWORD:

*(Calmly and concerned)* Sister, repent. Just repent. Have a good week ladies. *(He rushes away before they can speak again).*

MYRTLE:

(Looking after him) Rev. Goodword looks a little tired this morning, don't he?

MAGGIE:

Not as tired as his wife's clothes. I get sick of seeing her wear that same dress every other week.

MYRTLE:

Well, it aint' from lack of money. Goodness knows they get enough of that. Maybe she's just trying to look poor and humble.

MAGGIE:

Well alls I can say is she's doing a super good job. If he's tired, and believe you me, and I got this from a good source, it's not from staying home looking at her…if you know what I mean.

MYRTLE:

(Calling offstage to her children) Jessie Mae!!! Quit standing around yapping wid yo triflin' self and gowan home and git dinner started. Well girl, let me tell you what I heard. His car's been parked outside Bitter's house every night last week, and I know it's true. Now you know I check a rumor out 'fore I spread it. I went over there to see for myself. I tried to peep in the window but her bull dog mutt got after me. I ran so fast I betcha the Green Bay Packers would sign me up. (They exit)

SISTER WURSE:
(Who has been chatting with Sister Wrong) And you know she knew what she was doing when she stole your song.

SISTER WRONG:
I couldn't believe she did that.

SISTER WURSE:
She's been telling every and anybody who will listen that you can't sing. She even told the keyboard player that your voice makes him sound off.... way off.

SISTER WRONG:
WHAT!??!

SISTER WURSE:
I'll see you at the Tea, girl. Don't let those Johnston sisters stress you. (Exits)

SISTER WRONG:
(*Spotting Sister Goodword.*) Oh Sister Goodword, the programs came out so pretty. (Shows her one) I was able to get the exact shade of magenta that the bridesmaids dresses are.

SISTER GOODWORD:
Good! Good! After the tea this afternoon, we'll get the ladies to wrap them in satin ribbons. (*Elated*) Everything is going to be just wonderful! Now did you confirm with the music department regarding the songs Sister Biddle requested?

SISTER WRONG:
Yes. All of that's been taken care of . (*A little uneasy*) Uh Sis. Goodword, I don't want to be out of order, but there is a little something that's troubling me.

SISTER GOODWORD:
What is it? What is wrong?

SISTER WRONG:
Them Johnston sisters. They're a loose cannon in the church and all they ever shoot are missiles of discord.

SISTER GOODWORD:
Oh. Don't worry, Sister Wrong. God always allows a little abrasion in our lives to keep us smooth and polished.

SISTER WRONG:
They're not a little abrasion, Sister Goodword. They are a gaping, bleeding sore with pus and and venom and –

SISTER GOODWORD:
(Trying to console her) Sister! Sister, no don't say –

SISTER WRONG:
Maggots. That's what Maggie Johnston is, a maggot. A filthy slithering rotten stinking maggot. And her sister is a mean promiscuous man chaser that does nothing but abuse her kids.

SISTER GOODWORD:
Sister Wrong! I cannot receive your words. They do not glorify God.

SISTER WRONG:
What? You think that God doesn't know what Maggie and her sister are? Myrtle Johnston treats little Jessie Mae like she's a grown slave. That child doesn't even get a chance to do teenage things or have friends, or-

SISTER GOODWORD:
You're still complaining, Sister. Now don't let me have to rebuke you for the dark spirit of unforgiveness that's ruling you right now. Could it be that you are upset that she sang in your place today?

SISTER WRONG:
You think?! Of course I'm upset. Just pray for me. Pastor told her, when she was going on and on about nothing, that I was going to sing. There's a Brighter Side is my song and he likes the way I sing it. She had no right-

SISTER GOODWORD:

The glory belongs to God. Are you singing for Him or for Pastor?

SISTER WRONG:

I didn't get a change to sing for either one of them! And they imply all the time that there's something going on with Sister Biddle and Pastor. I am so embarrassed for you.

SISTER GOODWORD:

You're embarrassed for me? Do I look like I'm worried about my husband and any women in this church? My husband is a man of God and we must be righteous, Sister. We must.

SISTER WRONG:

These sisters are a disgrace to the Kingdom of God and I haven't said anything that wasn't true.

SISTER GOODWORD:

Oh, Sister, Sister. Come. Let us go and enjoy the Tea Party this afternoon. And give our precious Lord all of the glory.
*(Exit)*

**___FADE TO BLACK___**

# ACT I SCENE 2

## THE OFFICE

(Nancy Miller, rubs her head as if ill, yet still working feverishly, using a calculator, writing numbers, etc.when the telephone rings) (**2 phone rings**)

NANCY:
Good morning, Basil and Benjamin, Mrs. Miller speaking.......No, Maggie is not in Yet, would you like to leave a message?.....I.....don't know, I expected her at 9 o'clock ......(Grabbing an answering pad and writing) Yes....yes....o.k....yes, I understand. Play...what was that, 628 and combinate it? (Sighs) Yes. I'll tell her.

(Goes back to work when the phone rings again) (**1 phone ring**)

Good morning, Basil and Benjamin, Mrs. Miller speaking....Oh hi, Myrtle. No, She not in yet. Would you like to leave a message?.....Uh huh.. uh huh...(verbalizing as she is writing)...dreamed-9-6-3. Play it straight. Got it. I'll tell her.

(Hang up then picks up the telephone again and dials number)
Hello, this is Nancy Miller again.....Did Dr Myers get my message yet???... It's Urgent that he get back to me. I am in dire pain. Please keep trying. He can reach Me at my job....yes 555-6000. Thank you.

(Maggie enter with a coffee cup in a paper container, and does not speak. She sits down at her desk and unfolds the paper.)

NANCY::
Good morning, Maggie (No answer) You had some messages.

MAGGIE:
(Puts paper down slowly and glares at her) Is this where I'm supposed to guess who called?

NANCY:
(Reading messages) No, Ed Owens would like you to combine numbers 628 and Myrtle would like 963 played straight.

MAGGIE:
Is that it? (jots info down.)

NANCY:
Yes. Maggie, I took the messages today, but I'm sorry. I can't be a part of something illegal.

MAGGIE:
(Indignant) How dare you accuse me of such a thing! Not that it's any of your business, but they are ordering tickets for a play. As usual, you got it wrong.

NANCY:
Whatever. (She grabs her forehead with one hand and closes her eyes, wincing in pain.)
I'll be right back. I'm expecting a call from my doctor. (She leaves)

MAGGIE:
(Keeps reading the paper. The phone begins to ring as soon as Nancy leaves the room)
**(5 rings)**

NANCY:
(Running for the phone after it rings 5 times, she picks it up) Oh dear, the hung up. Maggie, I told you that I was expecting my doctor to call me. (Exasperated) I'm having trouble reaching my doctor. Now we don't know who called.

MAGGIE:
Well, what do you want from me?? You've seen the commercials, use star 69.

NANCY:

A little frustrated, but still gentle. That may not work with him. If that was his call that I missed, he may not be able to call back right away.

MAGGIE:

Look, quit whining. You said that you were expecting your doctor to call you. You didn't ask me to answer the phone. I just thought you were sharing useless information.

As I said, what do you want from me?

NANCY:

Maggie, please. I'm not well today. I'm on medication and my doctor needs to know

When I have reactions. So would you please answer the phone if I leave the room?

MAGGIE:

Who do you think you are telling me what to do? What you should be worry about if I have a reaction up in here. Why should I do all the work and answer all the phones?

Remember ? You got the bonus last week because the reports are your job.

NANCY:

Is that what this is about? Please don't stay angry about that. Mr. Benjamin had no choice but to ask me to do the reports, You refuse to learn how to do them last year.

MAGGIE:

Look! It's over! I'm a better person then you so I accept the things that I can change, and I ignore the things that I can not change. God has given me the wisdom to know the difference, so your little games are null and void around here.

NANCY:

I don't want to argue with you. Not today. If you don't mind, I think I'll take half a day off. I really don't feel well at all-

MAGGIE:

(Grabbing her purse and paper) Oh no you don't, girlfriend. Mr. Benjamin may fall for Your little illness trick, but you've got to do better than that to fool me.

NANCY:

I've already spoken to Mr. Benjamin. He is aware of my health and has agreed to-

MAGGIE:

I'm not feeling well myself. I'm sick of you. Goodbye!

NANCY:

(After Maggie leaves, she prays) Oh Jesus, please help me. (Holding her head) I know you're with me. Just help me to make it today, and deliver me.

(The phone rings again)

NANCY:

Good afternoon, Basil and Benjamin, Mrs. Miller speaking. Oh, Dr. Myers! I've been trying to reach you. It started … the pain is excruciating. I don't believe that I can drive right now. But I will go to bed as soon as I get home…..Hospital???? you've already called a cab for me? I will meet them downstairs right away.

(She exits weakly)

# ACT I SCENE 3

(Myrtle's apartment. Jessie Mae is seated and reading her bible.)

JIMMIE LEE:
(Out of breath, he collapses in a chair that has a small pillow) Ooooh! I'm so bored. (Jessie Mae does not answer) JESSIE MAE!!! (he throws the pillow at her)

JESSIE MAE:
Are you crazy? (Throws pillow back at him) Take Jonnie Mae outside and play.

JIMMIE LEE:
I don't want to. Besides, she's sad today.

JESSIE MAE:
Jonnie Mae, why are you sad? (Laying bible aside)

JONNIE MAE:
(Hugs her doll) I miss Mommie.

JESSIE MAE:
She's right in her room. What do you mean "you miss her"?

JONNIE MAE:
I miss her.

JIMMIE LEE:
She's on the phone.

JONNIE MAE:
Yeah, like always.

JIMMIE LEE:
Come on, let's play. (beats toy drums)

JONNIE MAE:
(Smiles)

JESSIE MAE:
That's a fun beat! Show me! (He shows her the beat) You need a song with this!

JONNIE MAE:
You can't sing to that beat!

JESSIE MAE:
(Cue Music) Sure you can. You can sing to anything!
*Sing to the beat of the drummer at hand Sing to the beat of a marching band*
*Sing to the song of the birds in the tree, sing to the wind and be carried alee*
*Sing for joy, for hope and love and sing for what you're dreaming of*
*You'll be free just wait and see be free be free be free just Sing and see*
*Sing from heart and the butter will fly, Sing with your faith and you won't ever sigh*
*Sing to the babe in the cradle at night, sing to everyone with all of your might*
*Sing for joy, for hope and love and sing for what you're dreaming of*
*You'll be free just wait and see be free be free be free, Be free*
*Be free (9 X) JUST SING AND SEE!*

MYRTLE:
(Entering) What are y'all doing in here? I could hardly hear on the phone. (Jonnie Mae tries to hug her. She pushes her away) Jonnie, you and Jimmie git on outta here messing up everything. (They leave) Jessie Mae, I need you to do another load of wash.

JESSIE MAE:
I'm getting ready to go to Sasha's house, we're practicing our dance.

MYRTLE:
I don't think so. I need you to babysit the kids tonight. Did you clean the kitchen?

JESSIE MAE:

Yes. I hate babysitting them; they never listen to me.

MYRTLE:

Well, assert your authority. You're the oldest. Did you pick up the groceries from the store?

JESSIE MAE:

Yes Mom. Why can't I go to Shelby and Sasha's house? I'm in the wedding party. We need to rehearse how we're going to dance at the reception.

MYRTLE:

I don't care nothing 'bout Shelby and Sasha Bitter. They's just like they Momma.

JESSIE MAE:

The name is Biddle. Why do you and Aunt Maggie deliberately misname people?

MYRTLE:

Cuz they's hypocrites, Baby. We just call 'em the way we see 'em. Now go help the kids wid they homework.

JESSIE MAE:

I've done everything that you've asked me to do. Why can't I do some of the things that I like to do?

MYRTLE:

Like what? Hanging out with riffraff?

JESSIE MAE:

Me?? You're dating Deacon Ladychaser and he has a nice wife.

MYRTLE:

Oh that ain't his real wife. They is common law which means he is free game.

JESSIE MAE:
Momma, we are Christians. That doesn't even sound right to me and I'm still a kid.

MYRTLE:
Precisely. Which also validates the fact that it's none of your business. Besides, I'm in love and love makes it right.

JESSIE MAE:
No it doesn't Momma. You need Jesus. He can show you true love. He can show you His love.

MYRTLE:
What do you know about love?? What have you been doing? You done been wid a boy?

JESSIE MAE:
No but I'm in love....I'm in love with Jesus.
(Sings)
*Each relationship left me empty, I was on my way to sin*
*But He reached down and touched me and saved my soul*
*And taught me to trust Him from deep within*
*One day, oh when I prayed*
*I found out true love when I fell in love with Jesus, Ooooo yeah*

MYRTLE:
*Well I've been going round and round in circles*
*And no one has show me true love*
*So I fell on my knees and I prayed for a man*
*I opened my heart and love walked in*
*One day, oh when I prayed*
*I found out true love when I fell in love with him* (holds picture of Deacon Ladychaser)

JESSIE MAE:
*He washed in His blood and covered me with love*

MYRTLE:
*He satisfies my needs where no one else succeeds*

(Together)
*Now I'll never journey in this life alone*
*He will always travel with me*
*And whenever trials may come my way*
*(JM) He's there, always, (M) he's there, he cares*
*Through eternity*
(Volley)
*I'm in love…I'm in love*
*He'll never leave me…He won't deceive me*
*He's mine…he's mine*
*I'm his…and I'm his*
*Ooooooooooh! Ooooooooooh!*
*I'm in love…I'm in love*
*Forever and ever forever and ever and ever….* (fade music)

JESSIE MAE:
Mom, I love you. And I want you to make it. Mrs. Nancy Miller died just like that! You've got to get right with God.

MYRTLE:
Nancy Miller? Are you sure?

JESSIE MAE:
Yes! She died. Mom, please let Deacon Ladychaser go.

MYRTLE:
Maybe, if I get finished first. But right now, I have to get ready for a date.

JESSIE MAE:
Well, can Sasha and Shelby come over here?

MYRTLE:
If it will stop you from whining, I guess so. What in the world am I going to wear? You think my white suit is too much for a casual dinner?

*Elaine Petry*

JESSIE MAE:
Don't make me any part of this relationship. You don't need my approval, although I feel like I'm the mother around here.

MYRTLE:
That's true. Cuz in about two seconds, you're going to be feeling a pain that's similar to labor if you don't get these clothes done..(Door Bell) And git the door!

MAGGIE:
(Entering) Hi Sweetie!

JESSIE MAE:
Hello Aunt Maggie. Take care. (Exits)

MAGGIE:
She's a good girl, Myrtle, but one sad child. What you doing now, want to go shoe shopping?

MYRTLE:
No. I gotta wait for Deacon Ladychaser to call. We got a date.

MAGGIE:
Oooh, he's bold. I been looking for Reverend Goodword all day. I need the church next week.

MYRTLE:
Well, did you call him over Bitter's house?

MAGGIE:
No, he's probably with Jack Miller. (Reading the paper) Nancy died you know.

MYRTLE:
I heard! Oh my goodness. She was just in church on Sunday. And she tried to take off Monday when you have to put her in her place. When did she die?

MAGGIE:
Monday.

MYRTLE:
Well, well what happened? Is it cuz you wouldn't let her go home sick?

MAGGIE:
Look, I had nothing to do with it. That's just life. Here today, gone tomorrow.

MYRTLE:
(*Children heard playing, laughing, and then a huge crash*) SHUT UP IN DERE!!! Jessie Mae! (Screaming) If you done let them hell raising demon siblings of yours break something, I'm gonna break you!

MAGGIE:
Girl, you'd better be careful. Your child abuse case is still pending you know.

MYRTLE:
(Taking a drink) These brats'll drive you to drink. At least that bum could have taken his brat with him when he left me.

MAGGIE:
Honey, you know it's a good thing y'all was shaking in a common law marriage, and that way, you cut out all the red tape you go through when you get a divorce.

MYRTLE:
And save a lot of money too. But you know what?

MAGGIE:
What?

MYRTLE:
I bet you anything in the world, Jonnie's daddy would have married me, bless his soul.

*Elaine Petry*

MAGGIE:
(Groans and rolls her eyes toward the ceiling in disbelief) HHMMPH!!

Myrtle:
(In his defense) Well, he certainly would have if he could have stayed alive. He was sweet, and kind, and a good provider, was a gentle mate and a---

MAGGIE :
(cutting her off, not being able to stand it any more) Myrtle, knock it off. He was a pathological killer, that stole everything he got his hands on, and he died in the same place he was born, the penitentiary where he was serving three counts of rape and murder !

MYRTLE:
(Twirling her hair) But, But, he, he, he, he,….

MAGGIE:
He got just what he deserved, the chair ! I WAS SCARED TO DEATH FOR YOU ALL THE TIME.

MYRTLE:
But he was good to me, Maggie . You got to give him that.

MAGGIE :
I'd be good to a fool too if I could get all his money and hide out from the law the way that criminal used you.

MYRTLE:
Well, I suppose I haven't had the best of luck with men. Jimmie Lee's daddy was the real rat in my life. He could squeeze the year off a dime, he was so tight. Jesse Mae's daddy was probably the right man for me, but I let him get away.

MAGGIE:
But you didn't even know who he was !!!

MYRTLE:

(Glancing towards the kitchen) Shhh!!! I was nothing but a teenager who had too much to drink that night. Jessie Mae's sweet so the father was probably a good guy, (hunching her shoulders) whosoever he was. Besides, that was sixteen years ago: I done asked forgiveness and prayed my heart out over that one.

MAGGIE:

Oooooh! And remember we fasted ? Remember I did it with you ?

MYRTLE:

Girl, you sure did, didn't you ? We fasted right though supper right on up 'til breakfast the next morning'

MAGGIE:

Uh huh! That was tough one.

MYRTLE:

So, I'm forgiven and that's all there is to it.

MAGGIE:

Well, girl, that certainly is all it takes. (Opens her paper and pulls out a pen) Ooh! I done found a woman in the obituary, who done died and left her poor grieving husband for me to find. (Laughs)

MYRTLE:

Oh! I almost forgot. What is this about Nancy Miller being dead !! But she was so young ? Whutn't she "bout out age ???

MAGGIE:

Oh no ! I'm sure she was much older than us. Listen, you can't get yourself upset. (Encircling another prospective mate in the obituary) Everybody got to die sometime.

MYRTLE:

Are you gonna go to the wake ?

*Elaine Petry*

MAGGIE:

I don't know. I guess, maybe,. Believe it or not, I hate wakes. Me and Nancy weren't that close. We weren't even friends. Matter of fact, I couldn't stand her. She was always in my face telling me what she thought a Christian should be, as if I wasn't living proof. Shoot. Maybe now I'll get some of those bonuses that are due me.

MYRTLE:

Well, it would look bad, after all she was a co-worker.

MAGGIE:

(Thinking) You know, I saw Nancy taking pills a couple of times. She might have been on drugs and OD'd or something.

MYRTLE:

Didn't you tell me that she took out an extra large insurance policy on herself? She must have known how sick she was.

MAGGIE:

(Perking up realizing pertinent information) Yes, that's right. She left it laying right inside of her pocketbook one day where everybody could see it.

MYRTLE:

Maggie, you didn't.

MAGGIE:

Well, she shouldn't have brought something that important to work with her. I*t was sticking right out of her pocketbook and (miming how she did it) I just kind of opened it and read it a little bit.

MYRTLE:

She must have really loved poor Jack and cared about his future to make that kind of provision for him. He must be very sad.

MAGGIE:

Poor Jack??? Poor Jack is a very rich widower. Poor Jack had 50,000.00 dollars to help make him happy. And of course I'll be right there offering and sacrificing my time to soften his grief. You know, that first month or two after the lost of a loved one that's when they really get lonely.

MYRTLE:
Meanwhile, are you going to the wake or what?? They didn't bury the woman yet, you know.

MAGGIE:
Now, do I look like the kind of person that would pass up an opportunity like this?

MYRTLE:
Opportunity?

MAGGIE:
Why, opportunity to lend support and to console poor Jack.

MYRTLE:
I'll go with you . (They laugh)

Lights Fade

# ACT 1 SCENE 4

*(Jack stands with his head down at the head of the coffin.)*

SISTER GOODWORD:
(Sister Goodword and Sister Wrong chat before the services begin) Oh that poor woman suffered so. But now she is out of her pain and with Jesus.

SISTER WRONG:
I heard that she passed away right on her job at the indirect indifferent hands of Maggie Johnston. At least I'm not the only one that she torments.

SISTER GOODWORD:
Sister! We should never repeat such things. And you cannot compare yourself to Nancy because she has left this earth and you are still here. And frankly, I think you torment yourself most of the time. Why don't you just stay away from the Johnston sisters?

SISTER WRONG:
You think that I go out of my way to have my songs stolen and feelings hurt every Sunday by that woman?

SISTER GOODWORD:
The Word says that we should put our affections on things above. You can't concern yourself with-

SISTER WRONG:
You can say what you want, but Maggie Johnston does not have another service to haunt me.

SISTER GOODWORD:
Examine your heart, Sister Wrong. Can you find anywhere in there to forgive her?

SISTER WRONG:
Forgive her? Why?? She's not going to change.

SISTER GOODWORD:
Then you change.

SISTER WRONG:
What!??

SISTER GOODWORD:
You heard me. I said you change. When you forgive her, you set yourself free from the discord with another saint.

SISTER WRONG:
No, I don't forgive some things. My ex tried to talk to me about getting back together. I said, no way! Some things you just don't forgive. If she was a true saint, then maybe, but–

SISTER WRIGHT:
Wait! Now let me get this straight. You just can't forgive some things. But yet, you want Jesus to forgive every sin that you commit. Unless of course you never sin. Unless of course, you're that true saint you're demanding from Maggie.

SISTER WRONG:
(Softening) Well, everybody sins at some time or another.

SISTER GOODWORD:
Exactly. Look at poor Nancy Miller. The precious dear didn't have time to say anything. She said goodbye to her loving husband one morning and he will only see her again in glory. Sister Wrong, we just don't have time to keep stumbling over the same mess our ancestors did. Time is truly winding up.

SISTER WRONG:
You've got that right, Sister Goodword. You are right. But let's not stand here. The Johnston sisters are coming and I don't want Maggie to wipe out all the sound counsel you just gave me.

(Maggie and Myrtle approaching. Myrtle is clearly distraught)

MAGGIE:
Girl, you've got to pull yourself together.

MYRTLE:
(Crying) I can't believe it Maggie. Deacon Ladichaiser broke up with me because he can't make a commitment right now. Well what does he call living with his wife? A casual acquaintance?

MAGGIE:
It probably is.

MYRTLE:
Oh, oh, oh, my little heart just got smashed in a million pieces. *(Weeping)*

SISTER GOODWORD:
Hello ladies. Be brave, Sister Myrtle. She was such a sweetheart. I'm going to miss her too.

MYRTLE:
Oh, I ain't crying bout her.

SISTER GOODWORD:
It's alright to cry, Sister.

MYRTLE:
Sister Goodword, I have the utmost respect for you as our First Lady. But right now *(aggressively getting in her face)* I need you to leave me alone cuz I can't be sponsible for what I'm-

MAGGIE:
*(Blocking her)* Oh, she'll be alright Sister Goodword. I'll take of her.

SISTER GOODWORD:
All right then. *(she approaches mic and sings* Rock of Ages)

*(Myrtle still tries to get herself together while Maggie threatens her)*

MAGGIE:
Now you listen to me. I've got an agenda here and I need to be focused. We'll mourn over your short lived affair with Deacon Ladychaser later. Right now, Jack Miller is swimming in grief and I'm gonna reel him in. So you straighten up and help me.

MYRTLE:
All right. All right.

MAGGIE:
(Noticing Jack.) Whew! Jack is looking soooo good today. I think black is his color. And of course, that $50,000 adds a right handsome glow of it's own. *(They laugh)*

*(As they near the casket, in view of Jack, Maggie begins to sob uncontrollably.)*

MAGGIE:
Oh my friend! My dear, dear, dear Nancy. *(Tries to climb into the casket)* We were so terribly close.

MYRTLE:
I know, Baby. I know. Let it out, Honey, just let it all out.

MAGGIE:
We were closer than sisters. *(She approaches Jack while Myrtle is shunned by Deacon Ladychaser when she tries to speak privately with him)* I'm so sorry Jack. *(She bear hugs him, turning him around and caresses his back.)* If there's anything I can do. Anything, Jack.

JACK MILLER:
*(Startled)* Th-th-thank you.

MAGGIE:
*(Approaches the mic seemingly grief-stricken)* It is such an honor *(She is interrupted by Myrtle's noisy sniffling, she starts again.)* It is such an honor to take *(Myrtle sobs as Maggie gives her a dirty look)* It is such an honor to take it upon myself to share these memories that I have of Nancy. *(Disturbing*

*the service and earning puzzled looks by the people, Myrtle sobs hysterically)* Can somebody assist my sister out of here please? *(Sister Goodword escorts her out)* I know how my sister feels cuz Nancy was a sweet gentle creature that was a delight to work with. Many of you may not know that we both worked for Benjamin and Benjamin Law services for many years and that I was the one who is responsible for her close walk with the Lord. (Sobs) We were like family.

She was the type of person that you don't mind doing things for. And I was always doing little things to her- I mean for her, just to see her smile. May she rest in peace.

*(She turns to Jack and hugs him, sobbing again)* Oh Jack, please remember if there's anything that you need, just call me right away. Anytime, Honey, anything. (Stops sobbing) An-y-thing. You just call me an-y time. Here's my numbers. (Pulls a card out of her bosom) My job number which you already got, my home number, my answering service, and on Tuesday nights I bowl. That's the bowling alley number on the bottom. And this here is my fax number, and that's my cell phone, which is also a pager. Oh and I got my own website. See here on the back, that's Hot-time.com. (She switches away.)

# ACT I SCENE 5

*(THE WEDDING. The wedding party dances in and parts for the bride and groom to enter. Afterwards, the bride throws the bouquet and Sister Biddle catches it. Maggie and Myrtle stalk her until she gives it to Myrtle)*

MYRTLE:

You giving this to little old me?? Why thank you.

MAGGIE:

(To Sister Biddle) It rightly belongs to her anyway. (they Sit down)

MYRTLE:

Honey, that wut'nt even a Christian wedding, and neither is this reception.

MAGGIE:

Girl, if I knew this wasn't going to be a Christian event, I wouldn't even be here.

MYRTLE:

(Gulping the last of her wine) Imagine!!! Serving liquor!!! Why, it's a good thing this wine is good for my blood pressure or I wouldn't even be drinking it.

MAGGIE:

Oh, Honey, the doctor ordered me to drink this here gin. (she pours from a bottle hidden in her purse into her and Myrtle's glasses) It helps me sleep at night.

MYRTLE:

Oh, Sister Bitter! It was a lovely wedding. And you lookted so nice!

SISTER BIDDLE:

Thank you, however the name is Biddle.

MYRTLE:

Right. Never seen you look that sharp before.

SISTER BIDDLE:
Thank you.

MYRTLE:
(on the side to Maggie) I can't stand her.

MAGGIE;
Well, I don't have no trouble out of her unless she starts telling me what the Lord done told her and what the devil done did to her.

MYRTLE:
She does me the same way. Every time I see her she say the same thing. (Mimicking her) "The devil works in many disguises, but wid some people he just have his way right out front. I just bind the voice of Satan. The Lord always tells me who he's using."

MAGGIE:
It would seem like some kind of spirit is always in contact with her, wouldn't it?

MYRTLE:
Honey, the only spirit she's talking to today is that vodka bottle. Look, she got it sitting right in front of her. I wonder what the Lord would say about that?

MAGGIE:
She'd probably say the devil gave her that.

MYRTLE:
Rubbish. Ain't nothing talking to her.

MAGGIE:
Well, if it is, it needs to tell her how to dress.

MYRTLE:
The dress is o. k. It's just three sizes too small on her. (Waves and smiles at Sister Biddle)

MAGGIE:
Well, at least she's not as bad as the daughter, the bride. Why didn't she just go ahead and have them make her a maternity wedding gown.

MYRTLE:
Really. Instead of trying to smash that baby with a girdle. (Belches, then sips more wine)
Ooh, excuse me. That food they served gave me indigestion.

MAGGIE:
And they had the nerve to top it off with coffee. They should have called it "mud in a cup".

MYRTLE:
I should have taken my little $5 and went to McDonald's instead of spending it on a wedding gift.

MAGGIE:
I'm sure we would have had a better time. (*A man approaches them and asks Sister Biddle to dance, to which she graciously declines.*)

DANCING MAN:
(Disappointedly) One of y'all wanna dance??

MYRTLE:
Wanna have your face slapped?? Wut do we look like? Can't you see that I could possibly be married? I ain't wid no husband, but you don't know that. I could still be married!

DANCING MAN:
I'm sorry, maam. I jus-

MAGGIE:
(Getting up, clearly tipsy) Well, I'm not married, but I'm a sanctified, born again, bible toting, Christian, and I'm filled with a spirit. You just insulted me and my sister.

DANCING MAN:
Ladies, please, I'm sorry. I didn't know. Honestly, I'm sorry. (He starts to back away when the music gets louder)

(SUDDENLY, MAGGIE AND MYRTLE SCREAM TOGETHER)

MAGGIE AND MYRTLE:
Oh, my song!

(They grab the man and dance wildly while the man is confused and dances in bewilderment. They toss him back and forth between them, bumping him and swinging him. Myrtle moves and gets a back pain while Maggie tries to help her)

DANCING MAN:
I've gotta get outta here….. (He runs away)

MYRTLE:
Maggie!!! Maggie!!!!

MAGGIE:
(Still swinging herself to the music) What's wrong?

MYRTLE:
I can't move. I done got stuck. (Maggie tries to pull herup) Oooh, I haven't danced like that in years. May the Lord forgive me.

MAGGIE:
Oh, I don't think He minds if we have a little fun. That's what Saturday nights are for, long as we're in church on Sunday. (they laugh and leave)

LIGHTS FADE

INTERMISSION

# ACT II SCENE 1

*(The next Sunday morning.)*

SISTER GOODWORD:
(Calling to her from a short distance away) Sister Wrong! I looked for you after the reception. Did you leave early?

SISTER WRONG:
I sure did. How are you this morning?

SISTER GOODWORD:
Oh I am so blessed. That wedding reminded me of what it's going to be like when we get to heaven. Just a whole lot of singing and dancing and praising God.

SISTER WRONG:
You thought that was a good wedding? Well, maybe it would have been if Maggie and Myrtle Johnston had not been there. They ruined everything as usual.

SISTER GOODWORD:
You think so? What happened because you were right at the verge of forgiving them the last time we spoke about them.

SISTER WRONG:
What happened? Didn't you see how they played football and tackled everybody for the bouquet when Shelby threw it? And they were drunk!! Where did they get liquor? Sister Biddle served nonalcoholic sparkling cider. I'll tell where they got it. They brought their own bottle!

SISTER GOODWORD:
Well, let them answer to God, not us.

SISTER WRONG:
And the dancing! Aren't you surprised that Sister Biddle had dancing at the wedding? Are saints supposed to act like the world?

SISTER GOODWORD:
Honey, the gifts belong to God. I believe in praising Him with what He gave us.

SISTER WRONG:
Maybe a real Christian could praise Him with the dance, but Maggie and Myrtle took it to another level. Those women are on their way to hell. I'm telling you! They are NOT saved.

SISTER GOODWORD:
None of us were born saved, Sis. And weren't you on your way to hell before someone prayed for you?

SISTER WRONG:
Yes, but I was a nice sinner. That makes a difference.

SISTER GOODWORD:
Not to God, Sin is sin. I was a crack baby. When I was six, my mother died by the hands of the man who raised me in the back of a bar, my father. They were fighting over money one night when he struck her and she fell down the stairs and broke her neck. He told me it was an accident and if I ever told anybody, they would take me away and give me to mean people. I believed him. Over the years, when the pimps, and the men, and yes, the women and the drug dealers could not supply what I needed, when the insurance ran out for the therapist I invested in, I thought slitting my wrist was the answer. But baby, my Aunt Lena found me. She told me that she had fasted and prayed for 30 days for God to show her where I was. She took me home with her, treated me like I was a princess and I gave my life to Christ. I was 18 years old. Somebody prayed for me.

SISTER WRONG:
Wow! I never knew your testimony!

SISTER GOODWORD:

You don't know anyone's testimony until they tell you! You should hear Pastor's! Somebody prayed for him too. So as far as Maggie and Myrtle are concerned, please pray for them. You can't sincerely pray for someone that you don't like, or if you are angry with them. Do you know that it makes YOU sin when you have bitterness in your heart?

SISTER WRONG:

But I'm right about them. You are nice. They are nasty and they're going to hell.

SISTER GOODWORD:

All the more reason to pray. All of us deserve hell. But do you know that I have never met anyone that I would like to see in hell. Have you?

SISTER WRONG:

(Pondering) Hmmmm! Let me think about that. Well, I could see Maggie plunging head first into hell when she tries to steal my songs and takes over like she owns the world. *(She does not see Maggie approaching behind her)* Yeah, I can truly say that Maggie Johnston can go to hell.

MAGGIE:

(Entering with Myrtle) You're right. I go to hell every time you get up try to sing. But don't hate me because you can't sing like me. You need to get over it and get on with your life.

SISTER GOODWORD:

(Stepping between them) Good morning, Sister Maggie. Hi Myrtle. Please don't take what you just heard out of context.

SISTER WRONG:

We were just saying that-

MAGGIE:

Oh you didn't stutter. I heard exactly what you said. It didn't phase me in the least. (Brushes them away with her hand) See ya! Wouldn't wanna

be ya! Sister Goodword, you's a first lady and you should really be more particular 'bout the people you taint yo'sef with.

SISTER GOODWORD:
I'm just praying that we all practice being more Christ-like.

SISTER WRONG:
You'd have to know Him first to be like Him. (She leaves)

SISTER GOODWORD:
Ah, Ladies, would you like to come to dinner today?

MAGGIE:
Oh thank you Sister Goodward, but I made plans already.

MYRTLE:
And I made dinner already.

SISTER GOODWORD:
My famous baked chicken with tarragon leaves will make you eat yourself to death.

MAGGIE:
Hmmmm! Yummy! But we've got to pass today.

SISTER GOODWORD:
O. K. Well, I'll see you later.

MAGGIE:
Bye! Did you hear what she said about eatin yourself to death?

MYRTLE:
Umm-hmm. Is her chicken that good? I never had it.

MAGGIE:
I don't know about tarragon leaves but if you eat it, you'll leave in terror, girl.

MYRTLE:
Waaaaaatt??

MAGGIE:
Sho nuf. I ate some chicken she baked one day and the doctor thought dat I had busted my appendix the way I fellup in dat hospital all bent over.

MYRTLE:
How in the world do you mess up baked chicken? All you do is put a little salt and pepper on it, put it in the pan and bake it. A blind one armed gorilla could bake a chicken.

MAGGIE:
That woman is dangerous in the kitchen. That's why Rev. eats like it's his last meal when he's not home. Did you see him wrapping up corn bread and putting it in his pocket at that reception?

MYRTLE:
No! Why would he do a thing like that?

MAGGIE:
He's hungry. Poor thing. Who could eat food like hers with a straight face?

MYRTLE:
I never knew.

MAGGIE:
Some things should stay hidden. Like her baked Terrorist chicken.

MAGGIE:
Oh, here comes Sister Bitter. Let's see which spirit she been talking to today.

MAGGIE AND MYRTLE:
(Sweetly together) Good morning Sister Bitter.

(turn):

SISTER BIDDLE:
(Indifferent) Good morning, Sisters. But it would be even better if you could remember my name is Biddle.

MAGGIE:
Right. All that hard work paid off. It was a lovely wedding. How you doing this morning?

SISTER BIDDLE:
I was doing fine. Negative spirits give me a headache.

MYRTLE:
Oh, you's gittin a supernatral headache is you?

SISTER BIDDLE:
It's not surprising. The Devil has a whole lot of church folks that he's proud of.

MAGGIE:
And that's a good reason to change churches. Umm-hmmm. That's jist why the Lord gave you that word to leave here. (Endearingly) Precious, I hope you received that command from the Lord I gave you last week. Cuz 'til you're obedient, you'll just continue to suffer in your body. It done already started with yo head.

SISTER BIDDLE:
(Looking up) Jesus, please deliver me right now.

MYRTLE:
That's a good start. Deliverance. I don't want to hurt yo little feelings, but I got to be honest. You need deliverance.

SISTER BIDDLE:
I have to go ladies. Between the headache and the disdain for nonsense, I actually feel nauseas. And I'm never in the mood to entertain Satan.

MAGGIE:
Well, you know how low down the devil is. But I'm sure the Lord will make you feel better soon. (A side hunch to Myrtle)

MYRTLE:
Bye! Y'all feel better now. (To Maggie) Headache? Wit dem blood shot eyes?? Honey, that was a class A, numbero uno, prime time hangover if ever I saw one. She jist don't know how to hold her likker.

MAGGIE:
It's a shame, ain't it? And that woman is gonna have the nerve to git up there and sing with the choir this morning after the way she carried on at that reception last night.

MYRTLE:
She probably didn't ask forgiveness for all that drinking she did. People are such hypocrites.
Oooh! My back is killing me. I feel like I've been run over by a Mac truck. Didn't that young man try to kill us last night? And us doing him a favor by even dancing with him.

MAGGIE:
Well, come on. Let's go to our seats. (They go into service)
Choir and congregants singing:

WHERE SHALL I BE WHEN THE FIRST TRUMPET SOUNDS
WHERE SHALL I BE WHEN IT SOUNDS SO LOUD
IT WILL SOUND SO LOUD IT WILL WAKE UP THE DEAD
WHERE SHALL I BE WHEN IT SOUNDS

(Repeat)

SISTER BIDDLE:
Come on, Church. Praise the Lord this morning. We've got something to be thankful about. We've got a mouth to praise Him. Come on, can't you praise –

MAGGIE:
(Cutting her off and taking the mic) I certainly can praise Him. You can sit down Sister Bitter.

SISTER BIDDLE:
It's Biddle. The name is Sister Biddle.

MAGGIE:
Biddle, Battle, Butter! From what I saw last night, it should be Sister Bottle. (to the church) That's a right private joke 'tween the sister and myself. You know, I done told Sister Bitter that she can't do it all. You got to give somebody else a chance to work for the Lord. She just tries to do too much and she gon tire herself out. so sharing that not of love this morning, I'll just give my testimony.

(Getting happy) I had a dream last night, and I just saw myself all caught up in a puff of smoke.

SISTER BIDDLE:
I know that's right.

MAGGIE:
It was cloud. It's my testimony, Sister Bitter.

MYRTLE:
That's right. It was a cloud. Go on Sister.

MAGGIE:
I was walking on that highway of gold. Oh, but you got to have a pure heart. A lot of you ain't gonna make it if your heart ain't right. Yes! Yes! I'm getting ready to get carried away here. Before I get too far gone, I'm gonna asj ny sister Myrtle, to come on up here and complete the devotions with a song for you. Come on Baby, do the best you can.

MYRTLE:
(Barely making it to the podium, she weak and feeble) Good morning, Church. Giving honor to Reverend Goodword, and his lovely first lady,

Sister Goodword, you look so gorgeous in that same dress, Darling. Church, I'd just like to ax y'all to pray for me this morning cuz Lord knows I'm in pain. The devil got out his directory of saints and went right to the Ultra Sain section, found my name at the top of the list, and just commenced to whipping me all cross my back and right down here through my hip section. He just want to stop me from calling on the sick and helping everybody. But I'm still going to sing for the glory of God, amen? Give me my key Baby.

(singing)

AMAZING GRACE HOW SWEET THE SOUND
THAT SAVED A WRETCH LIKE Y'ALL
I ONCE WAS LOST, BUT NOW I'M FOUND
WAS BLIND BUT NOW I SEE

REVEREND GOODWORD:
(Takes the mic from her) Right here is a good place for the offering. Please give your best this morning. Come on choir, give us a good offering song.

CHOIR:

(The offering basket is pasted down each row. Maggie and Myrtle each put $1 in the offering basket. Maggie takes change out – more than she put in)

REVEREND GOODWORD:
Father, bless Your name today. Use me in this place for such a time as this. Cause us to ingest, and digest Your word as we gestate and birth the purpose You have for our lives. We don't know if we will wake up tomorrow with the world as we know it today. Help us to lay down every dark thing and pick up speed as we finish the race, as we strive for the mark, as we rest in You. And every glad heart said….Amen. (Congregants repeat "Amen")

Church, turn in your Bibles to Matthew 24. The Lord is answering His disciples when they asked what shall be the sign of His coming. Verse 4 reads:

> AND JESUS ANSWERED AND SAID UNTO THEM, TAKE HEED THAT NO MAN DECEIVE YOU. FOR MANY SHALL COME IN MY NAME, SAYING I AM CHRIST; AND SHALL DECEIVE MANY. AND YE SHALL HEAR OF WARS AND RUMORS OF WARS: SEE THAT YE BE NOT TROUBLED; FOR ALL THESE THINGS MUST COME TO PASS, BUT THE END IS NOT YET.

> FOR NATION SHALL RISE AGAINSTY NATION, AND KINGDOM AGAINST KINGDOM: AND THERE SHALL BE FAMINES, AND PESTILENCES, AND EARTHQUAKES IN DIVERS PLACES. ALL THESE ARE THE BEGINNING OF SORROWS. THEN SHALL THEY DELIVER YOU UP TO BE AFFLICTED, AND SHALL KILL YOU: AND YE SHALL BE HATED OF ALL NATIONS FOR MY NAMES SAKE.

> AND THEN SHALL MANY BE OFFENDED, AND SHALL BETRAY ONE ANOTHER, AND SHALL HATE ONE ANOTHER. AND MANY PROPHETS SHALL RISE, AND SHALL DECEIVE MANY. AND BECAUSE INIQUITY SHALL ABOUND, THE LOVE OF MANY SHALL WAX COLD. BUT HE THAT SHALL ENDURE UNTO THE END, THE SAME SHALL BE SAVED. AND THIS GOSPEL OF THE KINGDOM SHALL BE PREACHED IN ALL THE WORLD FOR A WITNESS UNTO ALL NATIONS; AND THEN SHALL THE END COME.

(Excitedly) Endure to the End!!! Don't fool yourselves people. All of these things have ALREADY TRANSPIRED!! Don't think that you can still get away with your passive self-righteous hardened hearts. I beg you today. Be ready. If you have bitterness in your heart, admit it and throw it away. Yes they hurt you. Yes they wrong. But Baby let me tell you that if you don't forgive them, you're wrong too!!!

Endure to the end! Endure what? Endure being different. Endure being holy! Most of us would not embezzle money, commit murder, or a sexual sin or rob a bank. But we think nothing of withholding our tithes, telling that little white lie, gossiping about someone, having pride, or anger in our hearts.

Live holy! You many not have time to call on Jesus in the face of a catastrophe. You many not have time to whisper a prayer in the middle of cardiac arrest.

Live holy! Today, if you would hear His voice, harden not your hearts. Please. Please. While the choir sings, make your way down to this altar and repent! REPENT!! We may not have tomorrow.

(CHOIR SINGS)

REVEREND GOODWORD:
*(While the choir sings)* REPENT! REPENT NOW!!

SISTER WRONG:
(Sister Wrong makes her way down to the altar, with a few others. On her way back, she stops in front of Maggie)
Sister Maggie, I'm sorry. I'm just so sorry.

MAGGIE:
*(Looking past her as though she doesn't exit)* Well you should be.

REVEREND GOODWORD:
Repeat after me, church. Say "Father".

CONGREGANTS:
Father.

REVEREND GOODWORD:
Forgive me. I repent of my sins. Wash me in Your blood.

CONGREGANTS:
Forgive me. I repent of my sins. Wash me in Your blood.

REVEREND GOODWORD:
Make me ready for Judgment Day.

CONGREGANTS:
Make me ready for Judgment Day.

REVEREND GOODWORD:
You're dismissed.

(Congregants scatter, fellowship briefly)

MAGGIE:
Reverend Goodword! (His back to her) Reverend Goodword!

REVEREND GOODWORD:
(Reluctantly turning to her) Yes, Sister.

MAGGIE:
Reverend, I enjoyed that sermon so much. You're so good, Reverend. You put all of yourself into your messages. But you're looking a little tired. Are you getting enough to eat, Reverend?

REVEREND GOODWORD:
My wife takes very good care of me, Sister Maggie. And I'm glad that you enjoyed the service. I hope it penetrated deep into your heart.

MAGGIE:
Oh it did. You know, a lot of people are not going to make it in the rapture, but I'm glad and confident that I'll be there.

REVEREND GOODWORD:
Well, that's good to know, Sister. Excuse me. (He turns and walks dead into Myrtle)

MYRTLE:
(Returning to Maggie from arguing with Deacon Ladychaser) (She shakes the Rev.'s hand) Reverend Goodword, that was some sermon. Sinners (looking at Deacon Ladychaser) really needed to hear it.

REVEREND GOODWORD:
And some believers too, Sister Myrtle. Believers too. (He wrenches his hand from hers and leaves with his wife)

MAGGIE:
(Indignant) Well, what do you think he meant by that?

MYRTLE:
I guess he's talking about those people who think they're saved and they's not.

MAGGIE:
(Relieved) Oh, well then, he's definitely not talking about us.

MYRTLE:
(Reassured) That's for sure. (Yelling offstage) Jessie Mae!!! Git your brothers and go git that dinner started. Girl, it's really over 'tween me and Ladychaser. But that's ok 'cuz Deacon Pennypincher asked me out to dinner next week. But he's so cheap, I don't know if I want to be bothered.

MAGGIE:
He's more ugly that he is cheap. And he's a whole lot of cheap.

MYRTLE:

I know. He actually gives coins in the offering. Who can get tighter than that? Even I give a dollar every week. And I'm by myself with three kids.

MAGGIE:

People got to learn. You got to give in order to get. Honey, I give. That's why I get blessed everyday I go to lunch.

MYRTLE:

Lunch? 'Pacificly at lunch?

MAGGIE:

Yup. Everyday at Dino's Diner. I sit at the same table and Honey, the Lord just blesses me faithfully.

MYRTLE:

You don't say!

MAGGIE:

Sure as my name is what it is. Everyday I walk in that place, the money's laying right there on the table for me. I just got to be quick or the waitress will steal it.

MYRTLE:

I got to try that.

MAGGIE:

Well, I'd love to stand around chatting, but I got to go. (Absently adoring her nails). I'm fixing dinner for Jack Miller today.

MYRTLE:

What??? Girl, you'd better git out of town. How did you manage to pull that off?

MAGGIE:

Honey, I know what to do. I went on over to Dr. Buzzard's and he just gave me a little package to help sway old Jack my way.

MYRTLE:

He could probably help me git somebody, but I still owe him money. I'd better pay him before I be walking round here lame, crooked and looking out the back of my head.

MAGGIE:

Look, Honey, I've got to go. Remember now, the Lord taketh away, and the Lord giveth - me Jack. (They exit laughing)

# ACT II SCENE 2

*(Street.)*

(SOUND CUE) Lightning and thunder, screams and crashes.

JEFF:
(Mic in hand)Ladies and gentlemen, if you are able to receive this transmission! Report to the nearest fallout shelter. Hurry! Those of you that are left. Report to the nearest fallout shelter. If you are just tuning in chaos bedlam and catastrophic disasters have erupted everywhere. Men, women, children, and infants of every race and nation have disappeared from all over the earth into thin air.

A few members of our staff have been counted among the missing.

Some religions have threatened that Jesus would come back to the earth for believers but this has not been scientifically proven. I mean, I went to church and everything but I never in a million years really believed that this would happen.

People who were dead and buried have been sighted rising from sealed graves and tombs. This is the most horrific hoax that the terrorists have rigged in their history of torment.

Repeat! Those of you that are left, report to the nearest fallout shelter. This is not a test. This is not a test. (Breaks down in tears and runs away)

MYRTLE:
(Entering in total disarray screaming. She spots Maggie) Maggie! Maggie! Oh Maggie, I'm so glad to find you.

MAGGIE:
What in the world is going on?

MYRTLE:
(Crying) I don't know. I can't find Johnny, Jimmy, and Jessie Mae anywhere. Jessie Mae was giving the boys they dinner while I was on the phone with Deacon Pennypincher. The next thing I know, the line went dead, the children disappeared, and – and – and – (hysterically crying) Maggie, help me find my babies.

MAGGIE:
I was reaching to grab Jack and he disappeared right in front of my eyes. I never got a chance to lay a hand on him. (Sobbing)

MYRTLE:
What happened??? Where did the people go? Where is Reverend Goodword?

MAGGIE:
I just left there. He and his whole family are gone. I at least thought I would find Sister Goodword.

MYRTLE:
Well, (Sniffs) if the Reverend is gone, and the kids are gone, what made you think you'd find Sister Goodword?

MAGGIE:
The food was burning on the stove.

MYRTLE:
Oh.

MAGGIE:
(Realizing in shock) Myrtle. This must be the rapture when Jesus comes back for His people. Oh my, this must be the second coming of Jesus Christ.

MYTLE:
(Excited) Yes! Yes! This is it!! Get ready Maggie. Come on! Let's get ready!!

(Exit)

# ACT II SCENE 3

*(The Supernatural Realm.)*

(SOUND CUE) Lightning and thunder. (Enter the Angel with the Lamb's book of Life and opens it.

(Two angels stand ready to escort each person with a long flowing white chiffon fabric)

(As each soul comes forward to see if their name is written in the book, the Angel with the book checks off their name and points to either "Heaven" or "Hell". For those whose names she finds written they rejoice and go in the direction of Heaven. For those whose names are not found, a dark demonic figure comes and escorts them to hell.

ENTERING, ALL ARE DRESSED IN WHITE EXCEPT MAGGIE, MYRTLE, AND DEACON LADICHAISER. EACH SOUL DANCES WITH THE ANGELS AND PROCEEDS TO GET THEIR NAMES CHECKED IN THE FOLLOWING ORDER.

(Song) Joy to the World by Whitney Houston)

1. Jack - is met by wife after Angels 'passes' him.
2. Sister Wrong (Joyfully flinging arms)
3. Shelby (Looking for Jeff)
4. Sister Ladychaser (with baby in arms)
5. Deacon Ladychaser (Dances wildly. Goes under the veil but Angel with the book does not see his name. He offers her money then the Grim Reaper takes him away.
6. Sister Biddle (Flows gracefully)
7. Reverend Goodword (Leaps and jumps)
8. Jeff (wringing his hands and very nervous)
9. Sister Goodword (Glides and slides)

10. Maggie & Myrtle (Dancing until they get to the Angels. They are blocked, but they turn to the audience, wink at each other, then snatch the ends of the veil from the Angel's hands, encircle them, and tie them up. A warrior Angel touches them and they are freed. (Angels Dance – Richard Smallwoods Anthem of Praise)

The angel with the book holds up her hand to stop them from entering heaven. She can't find their names, closes the book and walks away.

MYRTLE;
Hey! Get back here angel girl. You're making a big mistake!! Now how do you like that? I KNOW my name is in the directory of saints.

MAGGIE:
(Thinking) Wait a minute. Remember when everybody disappeared?

MYRTLE:
(Confused) Yeah…

MAGGIE:
Don't you get it? We're still in the natural, the flesh! We ain't been caught up yet. This ain't even the right heaven. We're gonna see Momma.

MYRTLE:
Right! We gotta be caught up first! We are getting ready to get caught up in the air. Pure ecstasy. (Trying to fly) Can you see me? Am I still here?? Am I flying yet?

MAGGIE:
(Who has tried to fly, but stopped and is just looking at Myrtle) You're flying all right. Open your eyes. What about me? Am I glorified? Am I lit up?

MYRTLE:
You must be. I smell smoke.

MAGGIE:
This must be the rapture, with all these people gone.

MYRTLE:
It can't be. We're still here and if it was the rapture, we'd be caught up too, wouldn't we? (Looking at the audience) and there's others here with us too.

MAGGIE:
(In horror) Maybe, we didn't make it in.

MYRTLE:
Well, why not Maggie? We weren't that bad. We served on all the committees at church and never missed a service. (She gets angry at God and yells at the sky) It's not fair.

SOUND CUE: Thunder.

(Myrtle runs back to Maggie)

MAGGIE:
What are we gonna do now?

MYRTLE:
Well, let's pray, and maybe the Lord will change His mind. (Prays) Lord! Lord! (As if He's hard of hearing) This here is Myrtle. Myrtle Johnston. I've got my sister Maggie here with me where You done left us. Lord, whatever you think we done, you've got to forgive us and let us in. Now, now we can't be burning in no hell cuz we's both allergic to smoke. You try, Maggie, He's not paying me one bit of attention.

MAGGIE:
Lord! Lord! This here is Maggie. (Whispers) Jackson.

MYRTLE:
What's up wit that? Your name ain't no Jackson!

MAGGIE:
Well, Johnston is not real poplar with God right now.

MYRTLE:
Quit foolin' around and git on wit it.

MAGGIE:
Lord! Lord! This here is Maggie! (to Myrtle) Do you think I should mention your name?

MYRTLE:
Well, why not? I mentioned your name didn't I?

MAGGIE:
Lord! Lord! He ain't answering me Myrtle. Lord, I got my sister Myrtle with me. (she says Myrtle very low) Just like this woman said, whatever you think we done, you got to let us in. at least let me in! (Myrtle shoves her) It's probably because of all those kids you done had out of wedlock that we didn't get in.

MYRTLE:
Well, at least I had mine. You aborted yours!

MAGGIE:
(To audience) Oh no she didn't. Listen to me. Abortion is legal. That makes it right. And what about Dr. Buzzard and all that witchcraft you got me involved in?

MYRTLE:
Me?!!!??? You took me to him first.

MAGGIE:
Well, you the one who showed me the address.

MYRTLE:

(Furious) Well, let me show you this!! (She punches her in the stomach and shoves her) Now you get up there and pray – and pray right and git us into heaven.

MAGGIE:

Lord! Lord!! Please forgive us and let us in. Lord, I promise to be good now that I see you meant what you said about coming back. I done quit my cussing and swearing. And Lord, I gave up cigarettes just for you. Weren't you proud of me when I did that? Only thing, Lord is I did keep my gin cuz the doctors ssay it help me sleep at night and Lord you done made the doctors so I hope you ain't holding that against us. Lord, we promise to even be nice to old Sister Bitter if you let us in. Please Lord. Help me, despite Myrtle.
*(Both Maggie and Myrtle continue to moan and plead with the Lord to forgive them and let them in.)*

MYRTLE:

(Seeing the Grim Reaper approaching from behind Maggie)
Ma-Ma-Mag-mag-Maggie lo-lo-look be… They scream as they are taken away.

GRIM REAPER:

(Dragging them) AND THERE'S ROOM FOR PLENTY MORE!!!!

LIGHTS FADE TO BLACK

# KAYLEE'S DOLLS

## SYNOPSIS:

Kaylee's Dolls is a short skit that can be used to accent any occasion. It was written specifically to showcase a dance recital with children of all ages.

Kaylee's Dolls is a toy store owned by a widow, Mrs. Hanna Anderson. She and her assistant, Terri, are conducting an inventory when Lenny, a local employee of a dark and shady business, and his henchmen enter. Their intent is to frighten her into selling her store to the gangster proprietor to remove her from the community. She is neither afraid nor intimidated.

After she closes, they sneak back in to cause damage. When Lenny holds a match to a toy doll, the doll blows it out. He stumbles and hits his head while the men with him run away.

The dolls come alive and teach him a positive lesson of the selected theme. Integrated within the doll's teaching are songs and dance for any occasion.

## CAST OF CHARACTERS

### People
| | |
|---|---|
| HANNA | Owner of Toy store |
| TERRI | Store sales associate |
| LENNY | Good guy gone bad |
| MISS LIZZIE | Good Christian lady in choir |
| CHOIR | Singers |
| HAWK | Big time gangster. Owns a neighborhood of stores, and wants Hanna gone |
| HENCHMAN | Shadows Lenny |
| HENCHMAN | Shadows Lenny |

### Dolls
| | |
|---|---|
| CANDY | Singing Doll – Mistrusts people |
| TUNES | Singing Doll |
| CHORDS | Spoken Word doll – robotic |
| KEYS | Cute little doll who sings |
| BABY M | Infant doll |
| SARGE | Army doll |

### Other Toys
| | |
|---|---|
| Box of Crayons | Sings to Lenny "Color You Me" |
| Crayons | Follow Box |
| Singing Bees | Sings "Dance and Sing" |

# ACT I SCENE 1

(On the street)
It's the Christmas season. Carolers sing carols outside of the store. (Silent Night) Lenny and his henchmen enter at the end of the song. They harass the singers and they leave hurriedly except for one elderly woman.

MISS LIZZIE:
You're going to hell, Lenny Leach. You know that your Momma raised you better than this.

LENNY:
Miss Lizzie! I didn't recognize you.

MISS LIZZIE:
That's cuz you're on the road to destruction. But Lenny, it's not too late. Change your ways before your ways change you. (She starts to leave)

LENNY:
Yes, ma'am. You take care now. Save me one of them Christmas pies you make!

MISS LIZZIE:
(Turning back) You're a good man. You're just hooked up with the wrong people. Come on back to church.

LENNY:
I will. Just pray for me Miss Lizzy. (Henchmen look at each other.) (To henchmen) What? (They cower)

They leave. (Lights fade on street)

# ACT I SCENE 2

(Inside the doll store. Hanna is on the phone)

HANNA:
But this is the second time that I'm letting you know that I didn't get the shipment. And this is the third time that a shipment has been lost. I secured a post office box after the first time. Why do you keep delivering the order to the store? You must remove the charge from my account...... Well I'm not paying for something that I did not get.......I don't care who's signature was on your delivery, because there was no delivery here!......... Send it to the post office box as I requested.........Thank you.

TERRI:
(Enter stage left with a clearance sign) Hanna, do you want all of these dolls for the Christmas special?

HANNA:
Yes. They're beautiful aren't they? They belonged to my daughter, Kaylee when she was a little girl. She donated them to the store.

TERRI:
Really?

HANNA:
Yes. As a matter of fact, they are the reason I opened the store. I called it KAYLEE'S DOLLS. Kaylee always treated them as if they were alive.

TERRI:
(She picks up the sale sign that has fallen off the doll, Candy) She doesn't want to be on sale. She keeps knocking the sign off.

HANNA:
They do seem alive don't they?

LENNY:

(Sinister music) (Entering with two henchmen) Good afternoon, Ladies.

TERRI:

(Clearly frightened) M-M-Ma-Ma May I he-help you?

LENNY:

What a pretty little thing you are. (He leans close to her) Boo! (Terri gasps)

HANNA:

(Stepping between him and Terri) Oh, Lenny really. Stop being such a bully. What do you want? (To his henchmen) And you! Go stand in the back. You're scaring away customers. (They move as ordered.)

LENNY:

Easy. T'is the season to be jolly. Come on, Hanna, you know what he wants. I don't know why you're being so stubborn about it.

HANNA:

I'm not selling my store to Hawk, your gangster boss. And I'm not in the mood to talk about it anymore. You can tell Hawk to fly off the Brooklyn Bridge without his wings.

LENNY:

(Softening) It's in your favor. What's it going to take, Hanna –

HANNA:

Mrs. Anderson to you. We're not close enough for you to call me by my first name.

LENNY:

I'll buy your dolls myself. Just leave this area because I don't want anything to happen to you. I-

HANNA:

Is that a threat? Are you threatening me?

LENNY:
No, no! I just –

HANNA:
Get out! If you're not buying anything, we have a lot of work to do. (They leave) What nerve.

TERRI:
It's late. Do you want me to finish inventory tonight?

HANNA:
No, let's close up. I want to check to see if the Post Office got my order. (They prepare to leave)

TERRI:
Those thugs probably got your order.

HANNA:
Oh my goodness. You are probably right, Terri. I bet you anything they have been confiscating my shipments.

TERRI:
Yeah, and they're stuffing the dolls with drugs.

HANNA:
I wouldn't put it past Hawk. (Fade to black)

(Night setting) (Lenny stealthily creeps back into the store with a search light. He pours gasoline on Candy and opens a safety lighter. Candy blows it out. He tries again. Candy blows it out.)

LENNY:
What the-

(She pushes him and he stumbles, falls and hits his head on the floor. MUSIC. He is briefly unconscious and awakens confused)

CHORDS:
(Spoken word....DAYS OF THE WEEK) What were you doing?

LENNY:
(Rubs his head) Ow!

CHORDS:
Are you ok? Do you feel ok?

LENNY:
How do you think I feel? I was attacked by a doll. And I'm talking to a doll. (Becoming lucid) Oh my God! I'm talking to a doll!!

CHORDS:
I think you should be more alarmed that a doll is talking to you!

KEYS:
Should we kill him?

SARGE:
We may have to. We'll decide after the interrogation.

TUNES:
Come on Sarge. Keys! We don't do things like that! It's Christmas remember? A time for love and joy.

KEYS:
Yeah, I guess so.

CHORDS:
Of course it is. And Mr. Lenny. You really ain't that bad. You just work for bad people.

CANDY:
He is bad! He got stinking gasoline all on my clothes. (Brushing it off) Good thing for you that I am made of flame retardant material!

LENNY:
I'm sorry, Miss.

CANDY:
You should be! (He tries to wipe off the "gasoline") And keep your hands to yourself.

LENNY:
I'm in a nightmare and I can't wake up! I'm losing it!

KEYS:
Just let God do for you what He did for us. Give it all to Him!

**DANCE:**

BABY M:
(To Lenny) Up! Up! Pick up me!!

LENNY:
You're kidding right?

BABY M:
(Beginning to cry) Up! Pick uuuupppp!!

KEYS:
Come on Baby M, don't cry. Let's sing a song. (Away in a Manger)

LENNY:
That was nice. (To clearance dolls) But some of the dolls look so sad.

TUNES:
They're sad because she's gone.

LENNY:
Who is gone?

ALL DOLLS ON STAGE:
Kaylee!

LENNY:
Kaylee Anderson? She's not gone. She just grew up!

TUNES:
Well, wherever she is, she will always be in our hearts.

### SONG – IN MY HEART

*Oh we know how it felt to be held in her arms, no other one could feel the way she did then*
*And she had the sweetest eyes full of love and of joy and we never thought those days would come to end*

*But here you are in our hearts but far, life has called and you just had to grow*
*How we long to touch your loving face, no one will ever take your place.*
*But here you are in our hearts but far, life has called and you just had to grow*
*How we long to touch your loving face, no one will ever take your place.*

*Oh we know you don't belong to us, you never did. You were only on loan for just a while*
*But we'll always have our precious memories, of your kisses your hugs and of your smile*

*But here you are in our hearts but far, life has called and you just had to grow*
*How we long to touch your loving face, no one will ever take your place.*
*But here you are in our hearts but far, life has called and you just had to grow*
*How we long to touch your loving face, no one will ever take your place.*

*I miss your smile, your sweet embrace. But someday soon we'll your precious face.*

*But here you are in our hearts but far, life has called and you just had to grow*
*How we long to touch your loving face, no one will ever take your place.*
*But here you are in our hearts but far, life has called and you just had to grow*
*How we long to touch your loving face, no one will ever take your place.*

Repeat - Extremely passionate and emotional…..(all dolls join in)

SARGE:
CUT IT!!! YOU PEOPLE ARE OUT OF CONTROL! FALL IN LINE! FALL IN LINE! PULL YOURSELVES TOGETHER!!

(Soldiers and others stand at attention)

LENNY:
What on earth did I do to deserve this?

CHORDS:
Plenty. You need to see that you're wrong about something. We're a child's world and you just can't destroy a child's world. We all dance and sing and bring happiness to others. Just like you probably use to do. You ain't seen nothing yet.

**DOLLS DANCE:**

LENNY:
I've never dreamed anything like this. But seriously, I'm ready to wake up now.

CANDY:
(Has been coloring) (Turning to him) Oh, you're not going anywhere. We want to get to the bottom of your treachery. This woman has been nothing but kind to us and all of the children in the neighborhood. She doesn't deserve the likes of you. I don't trust you. I think that you need to think a little brighter.

LENNY:
What?

CANDY:
Think bright. Shine light!

BOX OF CRAYONS:
COLOR YOU ME! (Words Elaine Petry, Music Leonard Carter)
*I was the first in Kaylee's past, to color the world with hue*
*I was there one Christmas morn sparkling bright and new*
*So don't you think you know it all, cuz I've got a tale or two*
*I can change the way you look at life, and how life looks at you.*

*You'd better get right and try to be nice-it's the only way you see*
*I can use a little red gold or green and brother color you me!*

*There is still a place in Kaylee's heart, A secret place called "Child"*
*And when you hurt the one she loves, it makes you mean and vile*
*But Christmas is a time of joy- hearts are filled with glee*
*And just so you can see my point- Brother I will color you me*
*You'd better get right and try to be nice it's the only way you see*
*I can use a little red gold or green and brother color you me!*
*I can use a little red gold or green and brother color you me!*
*I can use a little red gold or green and brother color you me!*

(The crayons will then throw red green and gold tinsel on him. When leaving, the Box has to chaste a little crayon who doesn't want to get in the box)

LENNY:
This is wild. This is wild.

CHORDS:
I have a question for you. I heard you say that you didn't want anything to happen to Hanna. Are you sure that you're handling this the right way? You could be hurting yourself you know. Did you know that she is a widow? Her husband was in an accident.

*Elaine Petry*

LENNY:

I know. (Bows his head) Kaylee was just a little girl when her husband passed away. I was there. I've always been there. I knew her husband. (Sighs) We called him Skip.

CANDY:

You did? You act like such a bad person. Why would Mr. Skip Anderson know you?

LENNY:

He was a singer and we traveled around together for a while. He thought that if you had any problems, all you had to do to be free was to dance and sing. That's why we called him Skip.

CANDY:

He's right. To be free, as free as a bee! That's what you have to do!

(Children) (From the Hypocrites) Dance and Sing
*DANCE TO THE BEAT OF THE DRUMMER AT HAND*
*DANCE TO THE BEAT OF A MARCHING BAND*
*DANCE TO THE SWAY OF THE WAVES OF THE SEA*
*DANCE TIL WE DROP JUST YOU AND ME*

*DANCE FOR JOY FOR HOPE FOR LOVE*
*DANCE FOR WHAT YOU'RE DREAMING OF*
*YOU'LL BE FREE JUST WAIT AND SEE*
*BE FREE BE FREE BE FREE JUST DANCE AND SEE*

*SING TO THE TUNE OF THE BIRDS IN THE TREE*
*SING TO THE WIND AND BE CARRIED ALEE*
*SING TIL YOU'RE HEARD ALL AROUND THE WORLD*
*SING EVERYONE WHETHER BOY OR GIRL*

***SING FOR JOY FOR HOPE FOR LOVE***
***SING FOR WHAT YOU'RE DREAMING OF***
***YOU'LL BE FREE JUST WAIT AND SEE***
***BE FREE BE FREE BE FREE JUST SING AND SEE***
***BE FREE BE FREE BE FREE BE FREE BE FREE***
***BE FREE BE FREE BE FREE BE FREE JUST DANCE AND SING!!***

LENNY:
That was great! (He joined in the song)

CANDY:
(Clearing mats) I just love those bees. They're as sweet as honey.

TUNES:
We all do. They are adorable.

LENNY:
All of this makes me miss the old days. When I sang with Skip….Man that was something…..

CHORDS:
Sing, Lenny. Sing for us! (All gather around)

SARGE:
Keep it short! Keep it tight. It's o7 hundred!

LENNY:
(Sings)
*"The Christmas Song"*

BABY M:
More! (Begins to cry)

SARGE:
Lock it up!!

KEYS:
(Soothes Baby) Shhh, Baby M. Here's your bottle. (gives her a bottle)

SARGE:
Quick! Everyone in place!! The sun is coming! The sun is coming!

(Dolls resume there place. Lenny sits in a chair and holds his head. He dozes off)

(Hanna Anderson and Terri enter)

HANNA:
Lenny! Lenny! What in the world are you doing here?

TERRI:
(Running to the phone) I'll call 911. (She grabs a baseball bat from behind the counter)

HANNA:
No, wait. He's hurt. (To Lenny) You maniac. Why are you here?

LENNY:
(Holding his head) Uh....I guess I fell.

HANNA:
You fell! Fell where? In the door? Because you had to get in the door before you fell on the floor. Is this your pathetic attempt to get me out? To sue me or to have me condemned?

LENNY:
You've got some interesting dolls in here, Hanna.

TERRI:
He's crazy, Hanna. Let me call the cops.

HANNA:

(Frustrated) What are you talking about, Lenny? How did you break in here? Why are you in here? I can't take it anymore but I'm not selling anything to Hawk Mason.. Terri, get some ice for his bruise. Maybe he got some sense knocked in him.

TERRI:

Hmmph! (She hands Hanna the baseball bat)

LENNY:

Hanna, I'm really sorry.

HANNA:

For what? That you didn't get away with whatever you were trying to do? And what was that by the way?

LENNY:

I broke in to burn the store down. I wasn't doing my job. My job was to scare you, hurt you, anything to make you sell. But I knew if the store wasn't here, they would have no reason to harass you.

HANNA:

Why do you care? Why do you care what Hawk does to me?

LENNY:

For Skip. The reason he was on the road that night was because he was coming to get me. I didn't have my car and asked him for a lift. I never knew why he took 48 though.

HANNA:

I do. He dropped Kaylee and me at my mother's house. You foolish man. Have you punished yourself all of these years for something that wasn't your fault? It was no one's fault, Lenny. That's why they call them accidents. It was icy and the city had not put down any salt yet.

LENNY:

I felt so bad. I thought that I took a man from his wife and baby right at Christmas time. So I took the job with Hawk just to be near you. And when the neighborhood went bad, I couldn't leave you. Hawk starting eyeing this place for no reason. He's tied in with so many politicians, I can't understand why this means so much to him.

HANNA:

There is a reason. I got the letter two weeks ago. I was offered four times what we paid for this building. He had inside information that they are redeveloping this area and will buy up all of the buildings on this strip. I've already signed mine over to the city. That's why we were taking inventory. We're moving.

LENNY:

So he's too late! (Laughs) He's too late!

HANNA:

Yes. And if you had damaged my store and Kaylee's dolls, I would have to use this bat in the most unladylike manner.

LENNY:

You and your dolls are adorable Hanna Anderson. For a minute last night, I thought that they were real. That's what Christmas is about isn't it? They gave me hope and faith and made me believe in something other than myself.

HANNA:

That's ridiculous. You hit your head harder than you thought.

LENNY:

Let's go to the diner for coffee. You don't have to open for two hours.

HANNA:

That might actually be nice. Terri? I'm going out. Why don't you check our box at the post office.

TERRI:
Ok.

LENNY:
Where are you moving to by the way? I'm going to need a new job.

HANNA:
Well, Chords likes the city, but Candy would prefer the suburbs. She doesn't trust people.

LENNY:
Say what? (They leave) (Chords waves goodbye)

(Hawk surreptitiously enters. The dolls come alive singing. He runs screaming from the stage.)

SET
Photos by SILVER BRITTON

Cast and Director/Elaine Petry

TO ORDER SOUND RECORDINGS
Write:
Sisters' Circle Community Theater
P. O. Box 311
Freeport, New York 11520

Printed in the United States
By Bookmasters